The Cyrenius H. Booth Library
& Earlier Reading Institutions:
A History

Daniel Cruson

CYRENIUS H. BOOTH LIBRARY *and*
FRIENDS OF THE C. H. BOOTH LIBRARY

Newtown, Connecticut
2007

Grateful acknowledgement is made to Ray Shaw for designing the book cover and Ruth Newquist for providing the cover art; to Kaaren Valenta, Liz Arneth, and Kathy Beals for their assistance in final preparation of the manuscript, and to the Friends of the C.H. Booth Library for its continued support.

Copyright © 2007 Daniel Cruson

All rights reserved.
Any person wishing to quote from, duplicate, excerpt, or copy material from this publication must obtain permission of the author.

Cover Illustration courtesy of Ruth Newquist, NWS
Cover Design by Ray Shaw
Author Photograph by Don Brooks
Portrait of Mary Hawley by Sandra Wakeen

Printed by Bridgeport National Bindery

ISBN – 1-888006-21-8

To Andrea Zimmermann and Mary Maki, without whom this history would not have found its way into print.

2007 is a banner year for the Cyrenius H. Booth Library not only because it is a library of a "certain age" but also because it continuously changes and develops to remain a relevant and vital part of the Newtown community. Through its history, the library has proved successful in meeting the informational, intellectual, and entertainment needs that a growing and evolving town demands.

Dan Cruson graciously accepted the daunting task of researching and documenting the library's history and, in his inimitable manner, expanded the scope of the topic to include the history of early reading institutions which begins in 1876, fifty-five years prior to the founding of the C.H. Booth Library. Dan has crafted a fascinating story of the evolution of Newtown's modern library.

During my twenty-five years as library director, I've had the pleasure to work at the C.H. Booth Library with an excellent staff and a fine Board of Trustees. I saw the Friends emerge as a tremendous and effective volunteer force that brings "added value" to our library by sponsoring programs, materials, and technology.

Within all libraries great stories are to be found. Now, captured for all time, is the story of the challenges, failures, and triumphs of those who believed in the value of knowledge as well as free access to ideas and information.

Janet Woycik, Library Director

~ Contents ~

Chapter One - The Beginnings	1
The Nature of a Subscription Library	4
The Growth of the Collection and the Institution	8
Professor Charles Platt and the Library Renaissance	11
Chapter Two - The John Beach Library - The Library Matures	19
The Free Library Issue Revisited	25
Organizing the Collection	29
The Growth and Expansion of the Collection	34
The Library in the 1910s and 1920s	38
The Death and Replacement of a Newtown Institution	40
Chapter Three - The Sandy Hook Free Public Library	43
The Library Changes	45
Decline and Demise	48
The Zoar Library: A Historical Footnote	50
Chapter Four - The Cyrenius H. Booth Library	55
Mary Elizabeth Hawley and Cyrenius H. Booth	56
Building a Model Library	61
The Structure of a New Library	67
The Historical Collections	69
Chapter Five - The Middle Years	73
Alice P. Hancock: The Well Qualified Professional	74
The Library at War	76
The Post War Library	80
The Julia Brush Collection	85
John Angel and the Library's Magnificent Art Collection	87

The Sarah Mitchell – Betty Downs Years	92
Chapter Six - Expansion and Modernization	99
The First Expansion Attempts	99
Success	101
The Library Reorganizes	104
The Friends of the Library and Its Fabled Book Sale	106
The Antiques Reference Library	112
The Technological Revolution	114
Appendix	125
Index	137

Photographs

Marcus Hawley	3
The Red Brick Building	7
Professor Charles L. Platt	12
The John Beach Library about 1920	19
Arthur Nettleton	21
John Beach Library interior photo	23
John Beach Library about 1900	24
Rev. George T. Linsley	25
First library catalog	30
Catalog alphabetical by title	31
Catalog alphabetical by author	32
Cover of last library catalog	33
Civil War sword of Capt Julius Sanford	36
Rev. Otis Olney Wright	44
Mary Elizabeth Hawley	58
Cyrenius H. Booth	60
C.H. Booth Library, 1932	62
Library's reading room (right of entrance), 1932	64
Library's reading room (left of entrance), 1932	65
Mary Hawley's dining room furniture	66
Mary Hawley's bedroom furniture	66
Alice Carroll	67
C.H. Booth Library main hall, 1932	73
Alice Hancock Davidson	74
Gladys Dexter	81
C.H. Booth Library, 1945	82
Mary Lucas	84
Julia Brush	85
Sarah Mitchell	92
Betty Downs	95
Janet Woycik	96
Jim Kearns	106
Patron computers in reference department	118
C.H. Booth Library main hall, 2007	119
Library's reading room (right of entrance)	120

Library's genealogy room (left of entrance)	120
Young adult department, 2007	121
Children's story hour room, 2007	121
Side entrance featuring sculpture donated by The Friends of the C.H. Booth Library	122

Photo Credits

Except where noted all photographs are courtesy of the Newtown Historical Images Archive.

We thank *The Newtown Bee* for use of the following photographs: Alice Carroll, Alice Hancock Davidson, Gladys Dexter, Mary Lucas, Janet Woycik, and Jim Kearns.

We thank the Downs family for sharing its photos of Sarah Mitchell and Betty Downs.

And we thank Andrea Zimmermann for the photographs of the interior of the C. H. Booth Library as it appears in 2007.

~ *Chapter One* ~

The Beginnings

Widow Baldwin was dying. It was the spring of 1876 and Sarah Baldwin's husband, Caleb, had been dead for thirty-two years. They had been one of the most prominent couples in Newtown. He served as town clerk for an unprecedented forty-three years, even longer than his father, also named Caleb, who had served in that post for thirty-five years previous. Sarah and Caleb were literate people, part of the town's intelligentsia, and by the time of her final illness Sarah had acquired a fairly extensive personal library for the time of over 100 volumes. Wanting to do something for the community of which she had been such an important part, it occurred to her that her treasured books could be given to the town to become the nucleus of a town library. In this way she would satisfy her philanthropic desires and be able to posthumously share the great love she had of reading.

Sarah Baldwin could not have known that at the same time that she was making plans for the disposition of her library, 100 librarians were meeting in Philadelphia "for the purpose of promoting the library interests of the country." By the end of the conference they had founded the American Library Association, formalizing a library movement that had been building for the previous two decades. One of the leading figures of this conference, and later a guiding light for the association, was Melvil Dewey. He would later gain immortality through his extensive work systemizing library procedures and standardizing the cataloging of library collections with the system that still bears his name.

Libraries, of course, predated the formation of the American Library Association. The impulse to gather written knowledge together under one roof goes back to the ancient world. Hellenistic Egypt had one of the most comprehensive libraries in world history at Alexandria. Even in the United States, libraries had an early beginning when in 1638 John Harvard bequeathed to a recently founded college 280 of his books along with an endowment. The college reciprocated by naming the institution after him. The movement to create libraries for the public was also early and had illustrious precedents in Benjamin Franklin's founding of a subscription library in Philadelphia in 1731. These early American libraries, however, were relatively small, and almost all of them were of limited access with a membership that excluded those who had little social influence or the money to contribute to the library's growth and maintenance.

After the Civil War, mass production technologies and cheap wood pulp paper brought down the cost of books resulting in an astounding increase in the volume of book production. Choices of reading material also grew dramatically as the number of subjects published increased. In addition, there was a tremendous growth of popular fiction. This growth, in turn, created a "need for guidance in appropriate reading matter." Librarians were trained to be in charge of the small accumulations of books that began to appear in small towns all over the country and guide the formation and growth of those accumulations. Unwittingly, Sarah Baldwin was at the cutting edge of this library movement as her books were accepted by the town and a group of leading citizens gathered to found Newtown's first library.

The group of men and women who would be the primary governing body of the library for the next twenty years gathered in the fall of 1876. The exact date is not known because during these organizational meetings minutes were not kept and *The Newtown Bee*, the chronicle of all events in Newtown, would not be established until the middle of the next year. It is apparent from the earliest minutes which survive that Ezra L. Johnson was the one who took charge of these formative meetings and became the first president, at least unofficially.

Johnson was a well-known and respected personality in town. Today he is best known for his historical writings which began in 1910 when he started to write long columns on various aspects of Newtown's history for *The Newtown Bee*. Always on the front page, they continued until his death in 1914. Subsequently, his wife Eliza Jane Camp compiled these writings and, soliciting subscriptions from the townspeople, published them in an edition of 500 volumes. This publication resulted in Johnson being considered Newtown's first historian. More importantly, Johnson was intimately involved in the town's educational structure. He served on the Board of School Visitors, a primitive board of education, for an unprecedented fifty-seven years during which he visited and supervised all of the town's one-room schools. His dedication to education made it a natural that he lead the library efforts.

On January 16, 1877, papers of incorporation for the Newtown Library Association were filed with the state's secretary of state and corporate status was granted a short time later. Meanwhile, a subcommittee was formed and by-laws and rules for operation were drawn up. The by-laws were formally accepted at a special meeting on May 11, 1878, even though the association had begun operating under those guidelines by the end of 1877. In December of 1877 the first annual meeting was held and Johnson stepped down as president, considering his job of organizing the library to have been completed. Taking his place was Marcus Hawley.

Marcus Hawley

Hawley is best known as the father of Mary Hawley whose benefactions to the town would include the present Cyrenius H. Booth Library. His service as an officer of the library was a foreshadowing of things to come. Less well known is his business career. Marcus Hawley was the son of Thomas Hawley, the founder of Hawley Hardware in Bridgeport. Joining his father in the business as a young man, he traveled to California shortly after the beginning of the gold rush in the late 1840s. His purpose was not to seek his fortune in gold, but rather to seek that fortune in hardware. He was one of the only men operating there who could conquer the logistics of getting essential hardware to miners in the goldfields. The substantial profits that he realized from this venture he invested in a new, rapidly developing transportation technology – the railroad. He was an early stockholder in the Transcontinental Railroad, but he also invested heavily in local Connecticut railroads. He not only invested in them but used them heavily. His obituary bragged that he had crossed the United States sixty-nine times. By the time of the library formation, he was probably the wealthiest man in the county.

He was also the busiest. The minutes reflect that he was absent for several special meetings in 1878, and by the annual meeting he begged to step down because of pressing business engagements. He was relieved by Daniel G. Beers, a founding member of the Newtown Savings Bank and a noted local lawyer. Beers served for two years after which Hawley was again persuaded to step back into the presidency to serve another four years. These two men, along with Ezra Johnson, who continued his close association with the library, were the ones who gave shape to the nascent reading institution.

The Nature of a Subscription Library

The new library was not a free public library. The debate on changing to such a library would rage until just after the turn of the century, but at this time the most critical issue facing the library board was how to fund the maintenance and expansion of the book collection. A secondary concern was that of finding a place to house the collection. The library association would not go to the town for funding. In fact, the idea of town funding never arose in the course of its financial discussions. The funds would have to be generated by the association itself, and the most direct way of doing that was by subscription, having the patrons foot the bill.

Subscriptions were structured in several tiers. The first was life membership. For the one-time payment of twenty-five dollars an individual would be entitled to withdraw books forever into the future. Since this amount of money was beyond the budget of most, a one-year subscription was offered for one dollar payable in advance, and lesser subscriptions could be obtained for six months (seventy-five cents) and for three months (fifty cents). Even these lesser subscriptions were not cheap since the average daily wage for an unskilled worker at this time was only one dollar. On top of the subscription fee, there was a ten-cent fee payable in advance for each book that was borrowed, so in essence it was a rental library.

These fees were part of the library rules set up at the time the by-laws were accepted. They also provided for a two-week borrowing period, with the option of a one-time renewal (unless it was a newly acquired work which was not renewable). Late books followed the modern practice of charging a fine of two cents per day. An interesting aspect of these rules was that they allowed the borrowing of only one volume at a time even if it was part of a set. The reason for this is not clear but initially it may have come from the small size of the library. The rule insured that one member did not monopolize sections of the collection. Also each member had to be registered with the librarian before borrowing any of the library's treasured volumes. The usual rules governing the replacement of defaced or damaged books were also in place.

The problem of housing the collection was an immediate one and it was solved at first by lodging the small collection in the post office. At this time the post office was located in the north end of what is today known as the Chase Block, near the flagpole at the intersection of Route 25 and West Street. At least twice a week the association secretary, Mary E. Beers, "opened" the library, or more precisely was present at the post office to register new members or subscribers, sign out their one book, and sign it in again two weeks later. By virtue of her position, Beers became Newtown's first librarian. There is no indication that she received a salary.

At the annual meeting on December 2, 1878, the position of secretary and librarian were separated and Charlotte Nichols was voted to become the first independent librarian. She was also voted a salary of fifty dollars for the next year. It was further voted that by January 1, 1879, the library collection would be moved to her house which was located on Main Street, south of the flagpole and diagonally across from where the Cyrenius H. Booth Library stands today.

This arrangement continued until November 4, 1887, when Mrs. Nichols resigned. The previous two years had been ones of diminished activity leading to general discontent on the part of the library board and this may have been the motivating factor behind her resignation.

The library collection, now being without a home, was the subject of an emergency meeting during which it was agreed that the association would rent the upper rooms of the Red Brick Building, which was just a few doors north of the Nichols' homestead. This building had been built in 1855 to supply offices for the town clerk and the probate court.

The Red Brick Building (now the Scudder Building) was built in 1855 to house the town clerk and probate court.

Before this time the town's land and vital records and probate documents were kept in the homes of the town clerk and probate judge, which were neither safe nor convenient. The town offices occupied the ground floor of the structure, but the upper story, which was open, empty and only used for occasional meetings, was separated from the offices and only accessible by an external stairway that went up the south face of the building. This was an ideal situation since library operations would not interfere with town business.

The board now had something that they had been looking forward to for the previous decade, "... a room fitted, comfortably lighted, and warm, supplied with leading daily papers and magazines where all could bring their books drawn from the library and read them if they wished without disturbance and where all could come in from surrounding [school] districts and spend a pleasant and profitable hour and feel that they were privileged to all of the enjoyment that such a room can give."

Now that the library was properly housed, a new librarian, Mrs. John C. Gay, was hired. Her initial salary was fifty dollars, as had been her predecessor's, but within a year the board felt that the duties of the librarian had increased with the maintenance of the new location and her salary was raised to sixty-five dollars. The library was still only open on Tuesdays 1:00 to 6:00 P.M. and 7:00 to 9:00 P.M., and on Saturdays from 1:00 to 9:00 P.M., but the size of the collection had grown sufficiently large that the librarian had to spend additional time processing materials and tending to the interminable record keeping.

The Growth of the Collection and the Institution

To the original donation of 100 books by Sarah Baldwin, another 129 volumes were added by various association members by June of 1877, so the library opened with a grand collection of 229 books. A year after the library relocated to the Red Brick Building the collection had quadrupled to 1,024. By 1895 it had grown threefold to 3,079, a size that it maintained for the next five years. The tremendous jump in the collection in 1895 is accompanied by a mystery. In the annual report for 1894 the librarian reported that the collection stood at 1,782. In the next annual report the collection had jumped to over 3,000 but only 117 books were reported as being added to the collection over the course of the year. Somehow over 1,000 books were added and were never explained in the records of the library or by *The Newtown Bee*, which diligently recorded the activities of the library in detail.

Many of the volumes that created the normal growth of the collection were purchased with the fifty dollar annual book buying budget, after having been selected by a special book committee consisting of two board members and the librarian. Frequently, however, books were given by individuals, usually members of the association, in a tradition that has continued down to the present. These donations helped expand the collection at a much faster rate than could have been achieved by the book budget alone. In addition, individual members purchased subscriptions to such magazines as *Scribner's, Harpers, St Nicholas, Frank Leslie, The Churchman,* and *Argosy*. Usually a subscription to the *New York Times* or the *Herald Tribune* was also donated. Unfortunately, the library's periodical holdings were the result of uneven donations. With the exception of *Scribner's* the appearance of any magazine on the library's shelves was solely due to the generosity of a benefactor and this generosity was often sporadic so that a continuous run of any one periodical was unlikely.

The number of members and subscribers to the library grew fairly rapidly to around sixty and remained at that level throughout the last years of the nineteenth century. Likewise the circulation rate rose to about 2,000 items circulated each year and also remained fairly level, fluctuating only 300 to 400 in any given year. In 1882, Librarian Charlotte Nichols did a detailed breakdown by category of the books that circulated for that year, giving an interesting glimpse into the reading habits of Victorian Newtown. The largest number of books circulated was fiction, mostly novels, at 646. Next was history with thirty-four volumes, travel with eighteen, biographies with seven, essays and poems with only four, and one volume fell into the miscellaneous category.

The growth of the collection as recorded in the annual reports appears to have been steady and continuous. Looking at other aspects of the institution, however, that was far from the case. From its inception until 1884 the library's growth appears to have been fairly steady or at least static in any given year. The year 1885 then appears to have been one of great difficulty. There were no meetings of the library board between the annual meeting on December 9, 1884 to the annual meeting two years later, on December 15, 1886. At the 1886 meeting the treasurer briefly noted that his report was to be, "... a very brief statement. No money has been paid out or received except the amount received by subscribers and the rental of books which constitutes the salary of the librarian. No books have been added to the library during the last year." (The salary of the librarian had, in fact, been reduced to thirty dollars for the year.) A few sentences later he notes, "So little interest was taken in the library this last year that it was almost impossible to do anything in the way of adding new books and we hope that the officers will have more encouragement to place the library in a position to do the work that it might do in a town like Newtown."

The reason for this sad situation can be summed up in a word – leadership – or rather the lack of it. At the December meeting in 1884, Marcus Hawley announced that the press of business necessitated his stepping down as president and his resignation was very reluctantly accepted. The man who was voted to replace him was the Rev. John Addison Crockett. He is one of the most interesting men in Newtown's history because of his eventual incompetence and his position at the center of one of Newtown's most sensational scandals.

Rev. Crockett arrived in Newtown in the summer of 1884 to temporarily replace Rev. Morris Wilkins as the minister of Trinity Church, while Wilkins enjoyed a year-long sabbatical in Europe. Crockett was a young, seemingly energetic minister, who quickly became involved in the community and instituted several initiatives within the church including a well-printed newsletter. Part of his community involvement was assuming the presidency of the library association in the wake of Hawley's resignation.

At this time Mary Hawley, Marcus' daughter, was teaching Sunday school at the church and in the course of her work became acquainted with the new minister. This acquaintance grew into a full-blown love affair which resulted in marriage under somewhat mysterious circumstances in the spring of 1885. It was a small ceremony consisting of only the bride and groom and Mary's parents, and it was held in a small side chapel of New York's Trinity Church on Wall Street. A few days later the newlyweds embarked on a honeymoon trip to Europe. The sequence of events subsequent to their embarkation is somewhat confusing. Within a few months, Marcus and Sarah Hawley sailed to Europe meeting their daughter in Florence, where she had become ill, and brought her home without her husband. She had apparently been abandoned.

The ensuing scandal, since it involved one of the richest heiresses in the country, echoed through the newspapers for weeks, but the family remained silent about what specifically had happened. Mary Hawley receded into a reclusive existence, rarely being seen in public. In 1900, after the death of her father, she realized that if anything happened to her, her errant husband would inherit her fortune so she filed for divorce and the scandal was renewed with frightening vigor as the story reverberated through the pages of the country's scandal sheets as well as the legitimate press. Throughout all of this she remained quietly hidden from view.

As with Rev. Crockett's marriage, his community and church projects also quickly died. The newsletter had only a couple of issues and other programs within the church likewise atrophied. As with the church, so did the library association suffer. After his election as president, he never called another meeting of the library board. Upon his marriage in June of 1885 and subsequent trip to Europe, the position of presidency effectively ceased, and no one stepped in to fill the leadership void until over a year after his departure. In December of 1886, the remnants of the library leaders finally began the process of reviving the ailing library's fortunes. Integral to this process was the personality of Professor Charles S. Platt, who was prevailed upon to take over the vacant presidency beginning ten years of enlightened and energetic service that was as successful as Crockett's was failed.

Professor Charles Platt and the Library Renaissance

Charles Platt was a native son, having been born to William and Fanny Platt in 1846. William was a very successful button manufacturer in the Botsford section of town who eventually established the button factory that, until 1926, stood on Route 25 just south of Deadman's Curve and across from what is now the Sand Hill Plaza Shopping Center.

Professor Charles L. Platt

For a while young Platt worked in his father's button factory, but his love of music soon pushed his life in a different direction and he became the music master of Newtown. He made his living by giving piano and music lessons as well as serving as the organist for Trinity Church from 1883 until his death in 1908. He became a member of the school board, the Men's Club and sundry other community organizations, leading him to a status as one of the town's most prominent people. With his talent for organization and his knowledge of music, he immediately began the process of resuscitating the association's dying fortunes and finances.

The first task was the reorganization of library personnel. Shortly after his election, Mrs. Nichols stepped down as librarian. Then for two years the position was held by Mrs. John C. Gay, but by 1889 Miss Abbie Peck became librarian. (She was extraordinarily popular, and her skills and energy served the library well for the next forty years until she retired in 1928.) With the resignation of Librarian Nichols, the library had to be moved out of her home and within a week the upper floor of the Brick Building had been rented and the books moved. Now that the library had been set into a new and more adequate home and was being served by competent personnel, Professor Platt turned to the financial problems.

When Platt became president the treasury had a grand balance of $61.50. Since his genius was music it was natural that he would provide musical entertainments to raise money. He used his students as performers giving them performance experience. On February 1, 1888, they put on the first Old Folk's Concert in the town hall, which was then located on what is now the front lawn of the Edmond Town Hall. The evening was considered a great success, realizing sixty dollars, almost doubling the association's treasury. A few months later a Second Old Folk's Concert was held which realized $122.00. This was followed by a Golden Tea in August with music and refreshments which took in $131.00, and a Library Fair at the beginning of 1889 which netted $133.00. In addition to music, dramatic performances, usually with musical accompaniment, were performed, such as the play *Dairy Maids* in early 1889 which realized a record $181.00. The entertainments were not all this successful; the *Musicale* of 1890 brought in only thirty-three dollars, but on the whole they consistently raised over fifty dollars. The balance in the treasury by the time of the annual meeting in December 1888 registered a substantial rise to $244.00 and three years later it had increased further to almost $450.00, a balance that would be maintained throughout the rest of the nineteenth century. Meanwhile book purchases had increased, almost doubling the size of the collection in five years.

By 1893, however, the pace of the revival was beginning to take its toll on both the professor and his wife. Their energy was single-handedly maintaining the association's fortunes. At the annual meeting of that year, Professor Platt announced that he felt there should be more general interest in the library and that both he and his wife could no longer bear the brunt of the work. The result was the usual response of any institution when challenged - they formed a committee. The committee was specifically charged with finding a way to engage more people in library affairs and to establish a more stable means of raising money. Within three months, the committee and the town found themselves split on the nature of a solution, a split that broke along the social fault lines of the town, which separated the east side of town, mostly Sandy Hook, from the west side of town, most notably the village.

The committee consisted of three men: Allison P. Smith, the editor of *The Newtown Bee*, Frank Wright, a *Bee* employee and town treasurer, and Rev. Otis O. Wright, the pastor of St. John's Church in Sandy Hook. The committee was slow in getting started, having its first meeting two months after being commissioned, on February 10, 1894. At that meeting Rev. Wright noted that the library only had fifty-five subscribers, there were no life members and that the funding was being sustained almost solely by the efforts of the Platts. His solution was two-fold: First, move the library to a building close to the Newtown Academy which at that time was located on Church Hill Road across from St. Rose Church. Here it would be closer to the population of Sandy Hook as well as being close to the academy whose pupils should be encouraged to associate themselves more closely with it. Second, the library should be free. The second proposition was rejected because that would mean town support and the other members of the committee doubted that could be achieved. They agreed on the first proposal however.

In the wake of that meeting, as the possibility of a move toward Sandy Hook began to be talked about in the town and letters began to appear in *The Bee*, Frank Wright and Editor Smith reconsidered Rev. Wright's suggestion and reconsidered their acceptance of it. At a second meeting in February, they agreed to disagree. There would be a majority report and a minority report presented at the next library meeting, which would be held on March 5. Meanwhile, as *The Bee* encouraged all Newtown citizens to become involved in this important debate, an anonymous letter appeared below this editorial which noted that the people of Sandy Hook do not use the library now, and moving it would serve no purpose beyond straining the association's finances to the breaking point and losing the interest of those who lived on Main Street, who would not want to walk the half mile to a new library, all of which would effectively kill the institution. *The Bee* headline for the next week noted that the meeting was the most heavily attended of any in the association's history. Professor Platt moderated a meeting with standing room only.

The crux of Rev. Wright's report was that the move and the creation of a free library was important and morally justified. The issue of a free library would be tabled and reappear in the next decade but the issue of moving closer to Sandy Hook raised some powerful emotions. In Wright's words, "We are poor people down there and work for our living; we need the use of this library without doubt; we are deep in the valley of ignorance. Sitting there under the shadow of the everlasting hills, and some of us perhaps couldn't read a book if we had them; but I am sure if we could have this library a little nearer to us we should want to get it honestly; and we would want our neighbors and friends on the west side and on the beautiful hilltops to condescend gracefully."

He went on to summarize the issue most succinctly as follows, "It is 1.5 miles from the Sandy Hook Bridge to Newtown Street and it is about two thirds of that distance to the Newtown Academy. The distance from Sandy Hook to the present location of the library renders it practically impossible for the people of that part of town to draw books. If the people of the Street [Main Street] are not willing to go half a mile to get books to read, why should it be expected that Sandy Hook people should go a mile and a half for the same purpose?" He summarized, "The sum and substance of the whole matter is this: Will the people of Newtown Street make the necessary sacrifice of personal and local convenience for the greatest good of the people of the whole town, for the great future?" The answer it would appear was "No!"

The sentiments expressed by Rev. Wright reflect a split in the town that had begun after the Civil War and still finds echoes today. The fracture centered on the railroad line that ran north - south through town. Those on the east side of the tracks were generally lower middle class working people whereas those on the west side of the tracks were merchants and professional men, generally upper middle class. This natural split was exacerbated as the Irish moved into Sandy Hook and became the bulk of the working class population. Things were made worse by the Irish affiliation with the Catholic Church whereas those on The Street were primarily Protestant - Anglicans and Congregationalists. So too in politics, the Irish were predominantly Democrats and the Yankees were Republicans.

This split functioned on several levels and frequently became acrimonious, as it did in the Gray's Plain School War of the same year as the library debate, 1894. In that split the Irish faction and the Yankee faction actually came to blows and the legal tangle lasted for several years.[1] The library controversy centered along the same fault line.

The library majority report is notable in that it ignored the issues raised by Rev. Wright's minority report almost completely. The majority authors did briefly address the earlier decision to move the library and stated that after careful thought and a canvas of the community, it was honestly felt "that the best good of the library and its future usefulness would not involve its being moved."

Essentially, then, the report consisted of four recommendations:

1. A member is to be appointed for every school district to canvass for subscribers and money if need be.
2. That an effort be made to have ten or more citizens contribute five dollars yearly for three years for the maintenance of the library.
3. That any teachers in any school in town on presenting a certificate from the secretary of the school board, be made honorary members and thus given free use of books from the library.
4. That children attending school in town should be allowed all the privileges of the library except voting, after payment of twenty-five cents a year.

The last two recommendations were set forward in the belief that teachers, having a large influence over their pupils, could use

---

[1] For an account of that war see Cruson, Daniel, *Mosaic of Newtown History;* Chapter IV.

this influence to get students involved in the library. Students, then, with inexpensive access to books, would consequently develop the habit of reading which would result in long term support of the library.

The meeting then voted to accept the majority report with the exception of recommendations three and four regarding the involvement of the schools. The reasons for this rejection are not given, but there is an impression in the reporting of this meeting that school involvement would not yield the expected results and therefore were not necessary. Regarding the first recommendation it was left to the library board to find individuals to canvass each district. The second recommendation was left with a new committee consisting of the two authors of the majority report and Principal Cliff of the academy. Since the ten citizens never materialized it is assumed that this new committee either did not succeed or never met. The press is silent on the matter. The number of subscribers did increase by fourteen at the time of the annual meeting, so the efforts of the board to solicit subscribers in the school district was partially successful. The number, however, dropped back to about sixty within another year.

At the end of the meeting, Rev. Wright was asked about the rejection of his minority report. He was not surprised by the result, but he, "… expressed his regret that the members of the association did not take a broader and more unselfish view of the situation." It is perhaps no coincidence that the next year a book club was formed in Sandy Hook under the guidance of Rev. Wright, and within two years it had evolved into the Sandy Hook Library, a free public library.

Over all, the attempt to strengthen the library's finances and support was minimally successful. The reports which were published in their entirety in *The Bee*, publicized the association and clarified the issues that it faced. The meeting also brought out a large number of Newtown's leading citizens who engaged in honest debate, but as the furor died down over the succeeding few months so did attention to the welfare of the library. In the long run, the only lasting result of the debate was a delineation of the split in the social and political fabric of the town. Here was one of several incidents in the late nineteenth century in which this split became very visible.

Professor Platt finally stepped down as president in 1896, ten years after he had been first elected. He was succeeded by two other community leaders who served for a single year each. By the fall of 1899, however, the fortunes of the library took a dramatic turn for the better as a result of a letter from Rebecca Beach.

~ Chapter Two ~

The John Beach Library - The Library Matures

The John Beach Library about 1920

At 8:00 on October 24, 1899, a large crowd had gathered in the library's reading room. The primary purpose of this special meeting was the reading of a letter from Rebecca Beach by Rev. George T. Linsley, the minister of Trinity Church.

> To the officers, trustees, and members of the Newtown Library association:
> In view of the ever increasing needs for larger and better library advantages in Newtown, and the many attractive such buildings recently erected in our neighboring towns, I wish to express to the association my desire to build a suitable and commodious structure on some lot of ground provided by you for that purpose and with the understanding that you assume its future care. In the event of your acceptance, I would like to call it "The John Beach Library Building" in memory of the five

generations of that name who have lived in Newtown. Further discussion as to the plans and purpose awaits your decision.

> Very respectfully yours,
> Rebecca D. Beach

Rebecca Beach was a lineal descendant of Rev. John Beach who was one of the most important historical figures in Newtown. He was called in 1724 to be the second minister of the Newtown Congregational Church, and was exceedingly popular among his parishioners. But over the next eight years he fell under the influence of Dr. Samuel Johnson, who had founded the Episcopal church in Stratford. In 1732, in a crisis of conscious, Rev. Beach resigned and went to England to be ordained an Episcopal priest. Returning to Newtown that same year, he founded Trinity Church and because of his popularity, many families converted from Congregationalism to join him. He also founded Christ's Episcopal Church on Redding Ridge and, up until his death in 1782, he preached in both churches every Sunday. His loyalty to the King of England, who was the head of the church, led him to remain a Loyalist during the Revolution. His influence was so great that Newtown and the eastern half of Redding became well-known centers for Loyalist sentiment. That same influence meant that the local Committee of Safety would threaten him but, because of his popularity, never took action against him and he continued to pray for the health of the king up to his own death. This was the man who would now be honored with a library building in his name.

For the library association, the next major task was to find a site on which to locate the building. For this purpose a committee was formed consisting of Rev. Linsley, George P. Sanford, and Arthur T. Nettleton. This is the first appearance of Nettleton in the library records. The year before he had become the treasurer of the Newtown Savings Bank, a position that meant he controlled the everyday running of the bank. This was the beginning of a long distinguished career in banking that spanned the entire first half of the twentieth century. He would also become one of the most influential men in Newtown and a guiding light in the creation of the Cyrenius H. Booth library in the 1930s.

Arthur Nettleton

Within two weeks, the committee returned with the results of their search for a site. According to the minutes, "A goodly list of places was the result of their labor, but owing to the location and prices placed upon some, the committee advised reducing the number to be considered to five of the most feasible ones." Rev. Otis W. Barker, the minister of the Congregational Church, and the donor, Rebecca Beach were now added to the search committee and the process of making a final selection began. After two weeks of labyrinthine debate, the final choice came to be a small 55 X 80 foot parcel of land at the head of Main Street just across from the triangular piece of land on which the Soldiers and Sailors Monument now stands. This property belonged to Elmer W. Fairchild and was located just south of his house. Mr. Fairchild offered the land to the library association for $1,000, but to sweeten the deal he offered a $100 contribution to the association if they chose his property. Interestingly, the parcel did not include the well which lay just across the northern boundary.

The members of the association unanimously accepted the committee's choice and then appointed the same committee to seek subscribers to raise the sum of money needed to pay Fairchild. By March 27, 1900, the committee had completed the task of raising subscriptions so successfully that they had $1,072 from one hundred subscribers, twenty-seven of which were non-residents. The association took possession of the land two weeks later.

Coincident with the money-raising, plans were being developed for the building and they were presented at the same March meeting. Grosvenor Attenburg of Astor Court, New York, had been retained as the architect and had drawn up plans for a building measuring 44 X 54 feet. It was to be a single-story building in the bungalow style with a spacious front entrance hall from which one would enter the main room of the building. To the right and left of this hall were two rooms that would serve as a reading room and a collections room. To the rear was the large main room which was convenient for lectures or entertainments, as well as a place to relax and read.

The only known interior photo of the John Beach Memorial Library

The cornerstone was laid on July 23, 1900 with great ceremony. The actual laying was accomplished by John Francis Beach, who was seven generations removed from his lineal ancestor the Rev. John Beach. He was assisted by his uncle, John Kimberly Beach, Rebecca Beach's brother, while she looked on. As the young Beach placed the stone in position, he was noted to say "I lay the cornerstone of this library in memory of John Beach," which made up in sincerity what it lacked in drama.

The Beach library as it looked shortly after it opened in 1900

Rebecca Beach was invited back on December 11 for the final dedication and opening of the completed building. Again there was great ceremony and *The Bee* dedicated almost a full page-and-a-half to it. Shortly before 2:00 P.M. the doors were open and the children from the North District School, which stood where the monument is now, trooped across the street and filled the two smaller rooms. The large audience room was filled with assorted dignitaries leaving only standing room for the other attendees. Rev. Otis Barker gave the welcoming address, which went on for a full two columns and he was followed by the noted Waterbury lawyer F. J. Kingsbury, a friend of the Beach family, who after admitting that he knew nothing about local history went on at length about all of the notable men who had come from Newtown in addition to John Beach. John Kimberly Beach was again on hand to give a formal speech of presentation that consisted of a detailed biography of his ancestor and the library's namesake.

Rev. George T. Linsley

At this point *The Bee's* reporter was apparently running out of energy and resorted to listing the other five dignitaries who addressed the crowd. The building was then formally turned over to the library association by Miss Beach, and she was presented with a "beautiful bunch of carnations" by President Linsley. Everyone then sang the Doxology and filed out of the building while eighteen of the honored guests adjourned to the Grand Central Hotel where they were fed and entertained by the association. Newtown finally had a true library.

The Free Library Issue Revisited

Within two years of moving into its new building, the issue of becoming a free library was raised again. When the library association was first formed in the 1870s, there was no question of it being free. Generally, such libraries were unheard of in America, and in a rural community that had a limited number of readers, it was presumed that any reading institution should support itself, hence the subscription library. By the last decade of the nineteenth century, however, with the backing of the American

Library Association, the idea of free public libraries was being rigorously promulgated.

The idea first bore fruit in the larger cities. A free public library was established in Los Angeles in 1889, in New York in 1895, New Orleans in 1896, and Brooklyn in 1897. So by 1894, when the association was setting up a committee to reinvigorate the library, increase its base of support and improve its finances, the committee seriously considered becoming a free library. In this it was actually in the vanguard of library trends, but it clearly recognized that such a library had to be supported by public funds derived from tax money, and the voters of Newtown were not likely to increase their tax liability for a reading institution.

By 1902 however, the situation in Newtown had changed somewhat. Besides having a new facility which the association wished to be used more widely, the town had also just rented the old Newtown Academy Building on Church Hill Road across from St. Rose Church and, by August 1902, officially had a public high school. The creation of the high school revived the idea that the base of support for the library could be extended by involving the teachers and students. That, in turn, led to a discussion of utilizing recent state legislation which offered grants of $200 in the first year and $100 in subsequent years to towns that had a free public library. This money had to be solely used for the purchase of books, and could not be used for the hiring of library personnel or maintenance. The result of the discussion as always was the formation of a committee to study the matter.

Shortly after its formation, the committee published a short column in *The Bee* outlining the issues of a free public library and inviting public input. That resulted in a public meeting during which many ideas were presented and debated. Then the results of the meeting and deliberations of the committee were put before the association at a special March meeting and there was further discussion. The committee further distilled that discussion into a series of four resolutions which it then put before the board for a vote on March 27, 1903:

1. This association will make use of the library free to all inhabitants of the town of Newtown, provided that the town will pass the necessary votes to establish a free public library and to make an annual appropriation sufficient for the maintenance of the same in accordance with the law of the state relating to public libraries.
2. That the association consider an annual appropriation of $225 as sufficient for the maintenance of that library as at present conducted and will agree for this sum to give the same service to the public as are given at present, namely two afternoons and two evenings a week. (It was assumed that the state grant for books, alluded to above would also be utilized.)
3. That the association will establish a distribution station in so many localities in town as may be required by the town, provided that the additional expense of transportation and the care of the books should be borne by the town.
4. That provided such votes are passed, this association...will make such changes in its by-laws as to put the management of the library and its affairs in the hands of twenty-one citizens representing the different localities and various interests of the town.

This last resolution recognized that if the town was going to be subsidizing the library, the private association could no longer be the sole governing agency. There had to be more participation by the voters of the town. With this resolution, the association was setting the stage for the board of the Cyrenius H. Booth Library in the 1980s when it moved the library's endowment to public funding.

Resolution three had been talked about since the considerations of 1894, but this was the first time that branch or satellite libraries had been considered seriously. One of the factors limiting support and use of the library was the distance that had to be traveled to get to the books, especially from the outlying areas of the town. This was before the automobile made all areas of the town readily accessible. To get from Botsford to the village was a considerable horse or buggy ride or a moderately expensive train ride after walking to the Botsford station and then from the Newtown depot to the library, a process that had to be reversed to get the desired book home.

The solution was to periodically pack up a selection of books and transport them by train to Sandy Hook, Hawleyville, and Botsford. These choices of location were dictated by the location of train stations where the books could be received. It was also hoped that the station master or his minions could do the minimal amount of labor necessary to administer the collection. The costs would then be primarily that of carrying the books on the trains. Although this idea was not adopted, it anticipated similar efforts during World War II made by the Cyrenius H. Booth Library in reaction to gasoline rationing.

The report of the committee with its resolutions was accepted, but it was voted that nothing be done at the present time due to the confusion in the current state of town affairs, especially its finances. Apparently with the new school expenses, it was felt that the townspeople were not yet in the mood to accept the conditions that would have been necessary to implement the resolutions, especially those concerning money. After the vote to effectively table the resolutions, the chairman of the committee, Rev. Linsley proposed that the library be made free to the students of the high school. On March 31 the board voted in favor of the proposal.

The idea of a free public library was never taken off the table during the remaining life of the John Beach Library. The town would not realize this literary blessing until the formation of the Cyrenius H. Booth Library was made possible by the generous endowment of Mary Hawley in 1930. The high school, however, was drawn into association with the library by virtue of the student privilege of free use of its resources. The next dramatic episode in the John Beach story would be carried out by those students.

Organizing the Collection

In early libraries, arranging books so they could be located on shelves was a problem that was not adequately solved until Melvil Dewey invented his card catalog system. For small libraries organization was not a big problem. The librarian who had organized the collection knew where everything was, and a small collection took very little time to browse in its entirety. As the collection grew, however, finding a specific book could be difficult and a full browse of the collection became increasingly more time consuming.

The early association tackled the problem of organization in the most expedient fashion, arranging them alphabetically. The collection was first divided into broad subject categories consisting of fiction, history, biography, travel, essays and poems, science, and miscellaneous. Within each of these categories the books were arranged alphabetically by title starting with Miss Muloch's *A Brave Lady* and ending with Mary C. Clarke's *Yarns of an Old Mariner* (in the fiction section). Under history the listing started again with *America Vol.1* by Mary Howitt and so forth. Once the books were arranged, they were each given a number running continuously from 1 to the last book without regard to the subject. In this way all of the 410 books that the library held in 1878 were arranged and accounted for.

A list of all the books in this arrangement was drawn up and then printed into a small pamphlet or catalog and distributed to all members and subscribers. Anyone else who wished a copy could then purchase it for five cents. Since the collection was arranged on the shelf in the same way as it was arranged in the catalog, and since all of the books had been numbered sequentially, once the borrower found the number of his desired book in the catalog, it was a simple matter to go to its proper spot on the shelf and retrieve it. As time went on and new books were added, small supplement sheets were drawn up and printed.

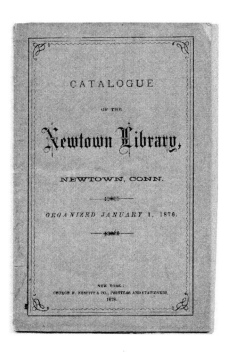

The first library catalog, printed two years after the Newtown Library Association was formed.

The first 1878 catalog is instructive in that it shows the complexion of the library's earliest collection. The largest category was fiction, numbering 185 volumes. Next came essays and poems with 58, biography with 46, travel with 36, and history with 32. Science was the smallest category with 12 and miscellaneous numbered 34. There was also a category called "statistical" but it had only one entry, *Manufactures of the United States in 1860*. Intriguingly, there were no reference books except possibly that last item. Generally reference books did not begin to appear in the collection until the 1880s. By 1897 there were still only six volumes given as reference including The *Encyclopedia Britannica*, *Rand McNally's Standard Atlas*, and *The Century Dictionary*. These books could not be lent out except under extenuating circumstances, and they were soon sequestered in their own location.

CATALOGUE.

FICTION.

1. A Brave Lady .... Miss Muloch.
2. A History of New York .... Washington Irving.
3. A Life for A Life. .... Miss Muloch.
4. A Mad Marriage. ....
5. A Noble Life. .... Miss Muloch.
6. A Princess of Thule .... Wm. Black.
7. A Wonderful Woman............. M. A. Fleming.
8. A Young Wife's Story .... Harriette Boura.
9. About Story-Tellers .... Donald G. Mitchell.
10. Achsah........................ Rev. Peter Pennot.
11. Among the Pines. .... Edmund Kirk.
12. An American Girl and 4 Years in College ..... Sola.
13. Annals of a Quiet Neighborhood.... Geo. McDonald.
14. An Old-Fashioned Girl............. Miss Alcott.
15. Armadale......................... Wilkie Collins.
16. Arthur Bonnicastle................ J. G. Holland.
17. Aunt Jane's Hero .... E. Prentiss.
18. Austin Elliott .... H. Kingsley.

19. Being A Boy.... .... Chas. Dudley Warner.
20. Blossoming of an Aloe .... Mrs. Cashel Hoey.
21. Boys of Other Countries .... Bayard Taylor.
22. By Still Waters.... .... Edward Garrett.

23. Cloverly......................... Mary Higham
24. Courting and Farming............ Julie P. Smith
25. Crusoe's Island................... J. Ross Browne

26. Daughter of an Empress............ L. Muhlbach.
27. Daughter of Bohemia.......... ...Christian Reid.
28. David Copperfield.................... Dickens.
29. David Elginbrod................. Geo. MacDonald.

First catalog listing alphabetic by title

By 1882 the number of supplement sheets made the process of finding books cumbersome as the searcher had to consult the catalog and then each of the separate sheets. It was therefore voted to produce a new catalog. This was also a time for a reorganization of the collection. The same subject categories were used but the books were now alphabetized by author's last name.

JOHN F. KEANE & CO., Successful Clothiers, 349 Main Street, Bridgeport.

A

1	When The Century Was New	Charles C. Abbott
2	The Land of Beulah	Mrs. Leith Adams
3	Home Influence	Grace Aguilar
4	Vale of Cedars	" "
5	The Days of Bruce	" "
6	The Scrap Bag	Louisa M. Alcott
7	An Old Fashioned Girl	" "
8	Eight Cousins	" "
9	Work	" "
10	Jo's Boys	" "
11	Little Men	" "
12	Little Women	" "
13	Stillwater Tragedy	Thomas Bailey Aldrich
14	Two Bites at a Cherry	" " "
15	Queen of Sheba	" " "
16	Ralph Wilton's Weird	Mrs. Alexander
17	Her Dearest Foe	" "
18	A Golden Autumn	" "
19	A Life Interest	" "
20	Blind Fate	" "
21	A Fight with Fate	" "
22	The Telegraph Boy	Horatio Alger
23	Ragged Dick	" "
24	Kelp	Willis Boid Allen
25	The Woman Who Did	Grant Allen
26	The Improvisatore	Hans C. Andersen
27	Only a Fiddler	" "
28	Vice Versa	F. Anstey
29	A Fallen Idol	"
30	Mansfield Park	Jane Austen
31	Sense and Sensibility	" "
32	Pride and Prejudice	" "
33	David Alden's Daughter	" "
34	Northanger Abbey	" "
35	Betty Alden	" "
36	Nantucket Scraps	Jane G. Austin

B

37	The Horse Fair	James Baldwin
38	Post Haste	R. N. Ballantyne
39	The Dog Crusoe	" "
40	An Historical Mystery	Honoré de Balzac
41	The Country Doctor	" "
42	Bureaucracy	" "
43	The Idiot	John Kendrick Bangs
44	Coffee Repartee	" "
45	A Border Sheperdess	Amelia E. Barr
46	The Squire of Sandalside	" "
47	Jan. Vedder's Wife	" "
48	Feet of Clay	" "
49	Remember the Alamo	" "

E. H. DILLON & CO., Fine Millinery, 360 & 362 Main St., Bridgeport, Conn.

1897 catalog listing fiction alphabetical by author

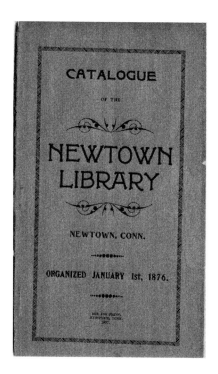

The cover of the last catalog dated 1897

As the collection grew to over 4,000 volumes, the system of alphabetizing had become exceedingly awkward. Fortunately, the new and superior system of organization developed by Melvil Dewey had become popular. At a special meeting on February 16, 1907, the board resolved that the library adopt the card catalogue system and classify books according to the Dewey Decimal System. It also resolved that Professor Jewel, the principal teacher at the high school, be put in charge of the work. It further voted to purchase cards and a card cabinet, provided the cost of the cabinet did not exceed twelve dollars.

The Dewey system did not differ from the old system in the way it organized books into subject categories. It did differ in that the new system put each book onto three separate cards, one for title, one for author and one for subject. These cards were arranged in the cabinet trays in alphabetical order. Then each book was given a distinctive number based on a master list of subjects drawn up by Dewey and the books were arranged on the shelves in numerical order. The book number also appeared on each of the three cards for that book. The card catalog was infinitely expandable. As new books were procured, the book cards could be simply slipped into their appropriate place in the card cabinet.

By the annual meeting for 1907 Professor Jewel, using his high school students, had typed up cards for all of the books in the collection. Parenthetically, this marks the first use of a typewriter in the library. The John Beach Library had entered the twentieth century.

The Growth and Expansion of the Collection

With the new building, the library became more popular. The number of subscribers doubled to over 100 by 1904 and people began to contribute more in terms of both time and resources. This, to a great extent, explains the rapid grown in the collection of book and other reading materials. Up to the opening of the new library building, books were primarily purchased, a sum of fifty dollars being allocated annually for this purpose. This meant that the collection grew by fifty to seventy volumes a year. Magazines were primarily donated and occasionally a single volume or set of books would be donated, but on the whole the growth of the collection was limited by the funds available.

Beginning in 1901, there was a major shift in book acquisition as substantial numbers of books were given by individuals. Starting in April of that year, Mrs. Oscar Dikeman gave an eclectic collection of twenty-five books ranging from a biography of William Shakespeare, and *Great Books as Life's Teachers* to Booker T. Washington's autobiography, *Up from Slavery,* and an unusual volume called *Flame, Electricity and the Camera.* By the end of the year, 113 volumes had been added to the collection by private donation as opposed to 93 volumes that had been purchased with an allocation that had been increased to seventy-five dollars. This pattern continued until the late 1920s with the number of donated books usually outpacing those that were purchased.

Another phenomenon accompanied the advent of the new library building, the donation of artifacts of Newtown's past. The first of these came in December of 1900. Mrs. C. F. Beardsley, who was living in the Baldwin House from which the original collection of books had come, donated the hearthstone from that house. On one corner of the stone a brass plaque had been fixed stating, "Ye olde hearthstone of Caleb Baldwin, 1819, presented by Josephine Lake Beardsley."

This was only one item of many to follow, some of which were somewhat bizarre. Mrs. Julia A. Chase, for example, upon her death in 1904, bequeathed a cup and saucer belonging to a set used by the family of her great, great, grandfather Rev. John Beach who, it was carefully noted, had died 121 years before. One of his sermons was also bequeathed as was a hand-painted Masonic apron that had been used by her grandfather Isaac Beach (1773-1822). It was duly voted that these gifts were to be kept on exhibit in the library.

A touching gift was Capt. Julius Sanford's sword. This was donated in 1910 by Mrs. S.S. Thompson of New Haven, the daughter of Capt. Sanford. According to the letter that accompanied the gift, the sword had been taken from Sanford when he was made a prisoner in Bayou Beouf, Louisiana on June 24, 1863. The inscription on the weapon stated, "Capt. Julius Sanford, Co. C, 23rd Regt., C. V. presented Oct. 1862, by his many friends in Newtown, Connecticut as a token of respect. Sanford was subsequently a prisoner at Camp Ford in Tyler, Texas for fourteen months before being paroled. He returned home and married before moving to New Haven where he died in 1879 of causes supposedly contracted while in prison.

The Civil War sword of Captain Julius Sanford which was returned to Newtown in 1910 has been on display in the John Beach and then the Cyrenius H. Booth Library ever since

The sword had been taken as a souvenir by Mont Hensley, a Confederate cavalry soldier. He was killed in March 1864, but the sword continued to hang in the family home for the next forty-seven years. Mont's Brother, Dan, was a postmaster in Ledbetter, Texas, and through the postal system contacted the postmaster in Newtown looking for Sanford or any of his descendants with the idea of returning the sword to them. This led to Mrs. Thompson and the return of the relic to her, and then to Newtown. For the rest of the history of the Beach Library the sword hung in a case on the wall with two brass plaques explaining the circumstances of its loss and recovery.

There were many other contributions to what became a burgeoning museum as the library continued to serve as a magnet for Newtown's heritage. On the dissolution of the Beach Library in the early 1930s, all of these artifacts were given to the new Cyrenius H. Booth Library where they became the basis of the library's extensive collection of Newtown memorabilia. Capt. Sanford's sword is now on display in a flat case on the south side of the non-fiction collection. John Beach's cup and saucer is on display only occasionally as is the Masonic apron. The sermon has not been seen for many years.

Beginning in 1910, another source of collection growth developed; the endowed memorial fund. In August of that year Austin Blakeman and his wife approached the library board with an offer of $350 which was to be used for book purchases in memory of their daughter Helen MacGregor Blakeman. Fifty dollars of that amount was to be used for immediate purchase of books that would "be suitable and of interest to girls." The remaining money was to be invested with the yearly interest to be used for further purchases and to supply subscriptions to the library as prizes for, "those scholars in the lower four classes of the Newtown High School who have the best standing each year, three in each class." Another condition of the gift was that the books were to bear a printed label "securely attached" that gave the name of the Newtown Library Association and the Helen MacGregor Blakeman Memorial Fund. Henceforth the annual report of the library bore a line item with the fund and the amount of interest generated or the number of books purchased.

Gifts continued to pour in, usually for one-time purchases, but by 1918, other endowment funds were beginning to be set up. In that year $500 was bequeathed by the estate of Abel Clark. In 1922 the brother of Sarah Juliet Hoyt established a fifty-dollar fund for children's books in her memory. That same year, the library received $1,000 from the estate of its neighbor, Elmer W. Fairchild, who had died the year before. He had been the one who sold the land on which the library stood for $1,000, so the bequest effectively fully rebated the purchase. The last of the major endowment donation was for $100 from Alice E. Briscoe. These funds added greatly to the collection over the course of the library's final two decades of operation. In 1928, on the retirement of Librarian Abbie Peck, who had served in that position since 1888, she could boast that over the course of her career, the collection had increased five fold, from 1,000 to 5,000 volumes.

These funds did not completely disappear with the dissolution of the Beach Library in 1934. Most of the funds were transferred to the Cyrenius H. Booth Library as cash and entered its general fund. The Blakeman and Fairchild funds, however, were transmitted intact to the new library where they continue to be used for book purchases to the present. The purchase of library subscriptions for top scholars from the Blakeman fund became moot when the Booth Library was constituted as a free public library, but the new library continued to serve young scholars in other ways.

The Library in the 1910s and 1920s

By 1910, the John Beach Library had established itself as a self-sufficient institution in Newtown. It still continued to have entertainments to raise money, but with the popularity gained by having a permanent home, came greater involvement by the public. To some extent this was also due to the growing popularity of reading and the further proliferation of popular fiction. The reading habit had finally penetrated even to the rural farming communities where advances in agriculture and basic homemaking made time more available for such recreation, especially for women. It is no coincidence that aside from the offices of president, vice president and treasurer, most of the other positions in the library organization were filled by women. These shifts were already well in place by the beginning of the second decade of the twentieth century and the history of the library becomes monotonously routine, with only a few trivial milestones to mark the passage of time.

One of these milestones was the arrival of electric lighting. Electricity was extended into the village from Danbury, over Stony Hill and along Mt. Pleasant in October of 1914. It did not penetrate into Newtown's outlying communities until after the Second World War in many cases, but where there was a concentration of residents who had the means to pay for the service, there it first appeared. Main Street, both immediately above and below the flagpole, qualified as the first area in town to be illuminated and the library, by virtue of its location, benefited from this.

At the annual meeting for 1914, the trustees were authorized to get estimates for wiring the library for electric lights. The electrification would proceed provided the money for wiring could be obtained by subscription and that the library was under no expense for having the work done. The subsequent minutes are silent on how the money was raised, but in the treasurer's report for December 1915, there is a line item for a Lighting Fund with the amount of $100. Below that were two other line item expenditures of $70.00 for electric lights and $3.30 for electricity. By the next year lighting expenses had settled down to $17.65 and the library could be considered modern by early twentieth century standards.

At 2:30 P.M. on Tuesday, March 22, 1921, a dramatic but less benevolent milestone was experienced. The roof of the building was discovered to be on fire, apparently from a spark from the building's chimney. It was quickly discovered, but there was a delay in getting water on it because the firemen could not locate a hydrant wrench. When the water finally started to flow, the blaze was quickly brought under control. The physical damage was confined to the south and west roof slopes, but most of the books on the shelves along the south wall were water damaged and the floor was flooded. By the next day, the damaged roof was temporarily covered and repairs were soon made, but the total damage was given in the next treasurer's report as $1,127.22, about one-eighth of the cost of constructing the building in 1900. The library was back in operation and a new supply of hydrant wrenches was secured by the fire company.

The last milestone, really a modest disaster, was the malfunctioning of the old coal-fired furnace in the fall of 1926. The verdict was that it had to be replaced, but because of the expense incurred repairing the fire damage of five years before, from which the association's treasury had not completely recovered, the money was not there for the furnace. A plea went out in *The Bee* for help and contributions were collected that amounted to $261. The furnace was replaced for $191 leaving a small balance that was apparently used for coal and some other minor maintenance chores. Beyond these events, the library continued to function in a normal quiet way until 1930 when the proverbial bombshell exploded that spelled the end of the association and the John Beach Library.

The Death and Replacement of a Newtown Institution

With the death of Mary Hawley who had become the town's benefactress when she donated the Hawley School and Edmond Town Hall, came the discovery that she had planned other benefactions for the town, which were to be bestowed posthumously. Among these was a new library building to be named after her maternal grandfather, Dr. Cyrenius H. Booth. Not only was the building provided for, but an endowment fund was also left to maintain it and supply operating expenses. The dream of a free public library was finally realized without imposing a tax burden on the non-reading public.

The John Beach Library now had competition. Over the course of the next year the number of subscriptions dropped by twenty percent and then even further the next year when the Cyrenius H. Booth Library opened its doors. By 1933, it was obvious that the association could not raise enough money to continue and that its services were truly redundant. At its annual meeting on December 11, the library board conducted virtually no business except to vote, "...that the Newtown Library as a Library, close January 1, 1934."

The passing of the Newtown Library Association was not to be as simple as just shutting the doors and walking away. It was a corporate entity with trust funds and other obligations, not the least of which was a memorial building that had been given to it in trust. All this required court action. Legal proceedings were begun in March and by October the Superior Court granted the association the right to pass most of its assets to the new library. The Blakeman and Fairchild funds were to be taken over by the Booth Library board and be used for book purchases as originally intended. The equipment and books were also to be transferred with the provision that what would not be incorporated and used in the new library would be sold and the resulting money would be put into a special line item in the budget called the Reverend John Beach Fund which would also be used for book purchases.

The largest asset was the building itself and that was auctioned off at the end of December. It was purchased by Edward G. Hadfield, a state trooper stationed at the Ridgefield barracks. It was understood by *The Bee* that he intended to remodel it into a home for his mother. The money realized from the sale was added to the other funds in the Reverend John Beach Fund. That fund continued on the books of the new library until 1978 when it quietly disappeared; the Newtown Library Association and the John Beach Memorial Library were now less than a memory.

~ Chapter Three ~

The Sandy Hook Free Public Library: The Other Library

As Rev. Otis Olney Wright returned home to Sandy Hook on the evening of March 5, 1894, in the wake of the rejection of his suggestion that the library be moved closer to Sandy Hook, he was struck with a thought that lifted his spirits. As the minister of St. John's Episcopal Church, he was in a position to offer the reading opportunities to his parishioners that the Newtown Street, Yankee establishment had denied them. He would start a book club. Money was not available in the lower middle class working community for the purchase of a collection of books and to provide for its maintenance, but almost everyone could afford to buy one book. What if after reading that one book, the purchaser passed it on to another member of the book club? If there were one hundred members of the club passing one hundred books around, among themselves, that created an effective library of one hundred volumes. By the beginning of 1895, just such a club was functioning guided by Pastor Wright. It had no formal organization and no overhead since the books were housed with the members.

The club was a great success. Within two years, it had attracted a number of gifts in addition to the books being purchased by individuals. So many, in fact, that housing them became a problem. For a while they were located in the church, but a more convenient location was soon offered in the old post office building. This building had been an old store built in 1831 at the corner of Church Hill Road and Glen Road where the Red Brick Tavern is now. In 1857, when William Glover wanted to expand the store, he moved the old wooden building across the street to the southwest corner of the intersection and made it available for post office quarters. The upper story was occupied by the Mason's and, on the main level, next to the post office, the new Sandy Hook Library established itself.

REV. OTIS OLNEY WRIGHT

Rev. Otis Olney Wright

By the beginning of 1905, Wright could boast, "The object was, and still is, simply to supply the wants of the public by cooperation. It is a mutual benefit. There is no fee; the use of the books is free. Everything is given: rent, fuel, furniture, and services. No one receives or asks for any compensation for anything." He then goes on to explain that most of the books have been gifts to the library, as were the magazines. What money is spent on books is donated. Books that have been purchased were done so at library prices and every transaction was recorded in a book that is open to the public. This was a free public library and Rev. Wright had succeeded in his desire to have a reading institution for the working classes.

Then on the morning of May 31, 1905, the fire alarm was sounded. A little after 3:30 A.M. Mrs. Nellie Tucker, who lived on Church Hill Road across from the Troy Hotel, looked out her bedroom window and noticed a red glow down by the Pootatuck River bridge. She phoned the telephone exchange in the village and the bell in Trinity Church was rung to alert the members of the Hook and Ladder Company that Sandy Hook was on fire.

The fire company, assisted by everyone in Sandy Hook who could help, valiantly fought the blaze, which burned uncontrolled along Washington Avenue from the intersection with Church Hill Road southward to the fifth building. At one point it was feared that the fire would jump the river and destroy the Niantic Mill, the large factory that stood at the base of the hill. Men stationed themselves on the roof and wetted it down along with the side of the building facing the fire. A line hose was run down to the Upper Rubber Factory, about a quarter of a mile away, and connected with a large water pump at the plant. Once that was functioning, the firefighters finally got the upper hand and the fire was brought under control just about the time that dawn broke.

In the coming daylight the damage rapidly became apparent. In addition to Hall's tin shop and two dwellings, the two-story former store that housed the post office, Masonic Hall and library was completely destroyed. Some valiant efforts by neighbors saved much of the valuable and historic Masonic regalia, and Postmaster Sniffen managed to get most of the post office valuables out so there was little material loss there. Miraculously, most of the library's 687-volume collection was saved and removed temporarily to the room over the Betts family store located at 113 Church Hill Road.

Within days, S. P. Glover announced that he would construct a new building to house the post office and library. The Masons had already decided to build a new hall on the opposite side of the road where it stands today. The new building was to be smaller than the old one, at 22 X 40 ft. and only one story, but the library at least had a home, one that it would continue to occupy until after the Second World War.

The Library Changes

Up until the fire, the library had remained informal. There was no paid staff, no officers, no by-laws or rules. It was run as part of St. John's Church with the greatest share of the work being done by Rev. Wright. The collection had started out small, but by 1902 it had grown to 362 with almost 100 volumes being added yearly. At the time of the fire, the collection had almost doubled and by 1917 the collection had grown to 2,500 volumes, the size it would remain until the library's dissolution. In 1902 there was a circulation of 2,250, which was comparable to that of the John Beach Library.

The institution had become an increasing burden on Rev. Wright, on top of his primary duties as pastor. Therefore, when the library became established in its new quarters, there was a move to diversify the workload and the first step in that direction was to incorporate. The library formally became the Sandy Hook Free Public Library Inc. on June 25, 1906. The process of incorporation, however, required some fundamental changes. The first was to have officers and by-laws so that the library now had to create some form of formal organization. A board of directors was duly formed and officers were elected. The position of librarian was also created so that someone would be officially in charge of the collection and regulating the circulation of books.

The incorporated library was still a free public library. Its free status, however, could only be maintained by keeping expenses to an absolute minimum. The building had been supplied rent-free and the fuel to heat it was donated as were the furnishings. All labor was volunteered. Magazines were supplied, as they were for the John Beach Library, through private donation. Book purchases, then, were the only expense and consistently one-half of all new acquisitions were also donations.

Beyond private contributions, money for books was procured by various entertainments. One popular form of such fund-raising was Whist parties. These were usually held in Glover Hall, which was a social center for Sandy Hook located on the east side of Glen Road. just north of the Glover Mansion (#1 Glen Road). In one successful event, ten tables were set up and filled with forty players plus there were a large number of onlookers. Both the players and onlookers were invited to attend and paid a small entrance fee. Those invitees who did not show, often paid the fee anyway as a donation. There were prizes for the high scorers, including such items as a box of candy, a knitted shawl, handkerchiefs both plain and lace-trimmed, cuff links, candlesticks, and in one case a toy rooster and hen. Most of these prizes also were donated. By the end of the evening, $15.25 had been realized and turned over to the library.

In later years, dances were held on Main Street at the Newtown Inn (located where the Cyrenius H. Booth is today). The price of admission was thirty-five cents and dancing to a live band or small orchestra began at 8:00 P.M. and lasted until at least midnight. A colonial tea and food sale was another fund-raising device. This was usually held in a private home which was decorated for the occasion and costumed ladies served tea and small sandwiches to those who had purchased a twenty-cent ticket. There was also for sale an assortment of cakes, pies, cookies, crullers, and bread. One of these teas held in March of 1922 filled Mapleton (7 Washington Avenue) with 150 people and realized seventy-five dollars.

Another feature of the Sandy Hook Library in which the hand of Rev. Wright can be clearly seen was the traveling libraries. These consisted of two types. The first was a collection of books that came into the library on temporary loan to augment the existing collection. The Leed's Traveling Library #20, for example, frequently rotated twenty-seven volumes into the library and a collection of thirty-two volumes of children's books were periodically lent by the Colonial Dames of America.

In the library as a whole, a great deal of attention was given to reading matter suitable for children and the second type of traveling library served this need. There were three or four of these and they consisted of twenty-five volumes that were sent to one of the district schoolhouses where they could be conveniently borrowed by its students. After a month or so, the small collection would be sent to another schoolhouse and a new traveling library would arrive a month or two later. In this way up to 100 volumes would be circulated throughout the school community to introduce children to the delights of reading. By 1905 some adult books were being included in the traveling collection. These were for the elderly members of the school districts, especially the outlying ones, who found it difficult to get to Sandy Hook.

Decline and Demise

By 1910 the Sandy Hook Library was established and functioning smoothly with its all-volunteer staff. For most of its existence it was only open one day a week; Saturday from 3:00 to 5:00 P.M. and in the evening from 7:00 to 8:00 P.M. but that was sufficient to give the people of Sandy Hook convenient access to books and magazines. What little money it needed for book purchases was usually supplied by a combination of entertainments and donations, but periodically the board of directors had to stimulate donations. When new books were not added regularly, borrowing declined and consequently donations declined as well. A peppy statement in *The Bee* from the board president was then needed to reinvigorate the flow of money.

Decline began to set in during the Second World War. With gas rationing, it became difficult to travel with any frequency to either of the libraries: Sandy Hook or the relatively new Cyrenius H. Booth Library, and both suffered. The first real blow to Sandy Hook Library however came right after the war when the small building that Glover had built for the library and post office was sold. The post office had been paying rent and so was allowed to stay until it eventually moved next door. The library, however, had been using the building rent-free, a situation which the new owner was unwilling to continue. By February 1947 it was looking for a new home.

That home came in the form of an arrangement with the Sandy Hook Fire Company. They had just purchased Glover Hall and were planning to use part of it as a place for its meetings. The rest of the main floor and the whole upper story was then open for use as a community center with recreation and meeting facilities for the Sandy Hook Athletic Club, meeting space for the local drum, fife, and bugle corps, and, of course, space for the library. The library was now set for the foreseeable future.

Six years later the foreseeable future came to an end. The equipment of the fire company had grown dramatically and space was needed to house it. By the end of January the library was informed that they would have to move out. This caused some consternation in Sandy Hook since many people had been of the same opinion as the library board that Glover Hall had been refurbished to be a community center and housing the library was part of any functioning community center. The meetings with the fire company were kept friendly and the company offered to help find another location and to help with the moving of books and equipment, but they were adamant about recovering the space for fire company use and storage.

Within a month the library had been shifted to the old grist mill that stood diagonally across from Glover Hall, but it never really survived the relocation. With automobile transportation common, Main Street and the Cyrenius H. Booth Library were no longer as inaccessible as they had been. A trip to The Street to find a book was only a few minutes' drive and the new library was a comfortable and attractive facility with more current reading material than its marginalized Sandy Hook counterpart could supply. As Caroline Stokes, who had been on the Sandy Hook library board since arriving in Sandy Hook in 1948, recently remarked, "It had simply outlived its usefulness."

The library closed and eventually the books were moved to the barn of Anna May Betts. Miss Betts was the daughter of Dr. Ralph Betts, one of Newtown's first dentists. She had been a school teacher and was very much involved with the cultural activities of Sandy Hook. When she retired from teaching she continued her strong involvement in the town's reading institutions, serving on the board of the Sandy Hook Library as its treasurer. She also was a charter member of the board of the new Cyrenius H. Booth Library from 1931 until her death in 1976.

Her last act for the old library was to join with Birdsey Parsons, who had been the final president, and hold the library's last board meeting on May 9, 1974. The only business of that meeting was a resolution to donate all of the library's assets to the Cyrenius H. Booth Library, a proposition that the Booth Library board had already accepted. Thus the resources of all the town's reading institutions were consolidated, and, until recently, books with the book plate of the Sandy Hook Free Public Library occasionally could be found on the Booth Library's shelves.

The Zoar Library: A Historical Footnote

The first mention of a library in the Gray's Plain District comes in October 1909 when Mrs. Mary A. Boyd, who spent the previous summer vacationing in Zoar, gave to Mrs. Frederick Bemis, "...a handsome bookcase, two fine pictures, also about ten volumes." Unfortunately no one bothered to tell *The Bee* reporter what the subject of the two pictures was nor what the ten volumes were. In the same reportage, President Hadley of Yale presented nine volumes, the Misses Chambers seven volumes, and Mrs. L. J. Wiley of Vassar thirty-eight volumes among which was a complete set of Shakespeare. A short time later, Mrs. Luzon Morris of New Haven, wife of the former Connecticut governor, donated seven unnamed volumes. All of the donors were residents or at least summer residents of the Gray's Plain and Zoar School Districts and Isabelle Bemis, the keeper of the library, lived on the line between the two districts. Even though she formally lived in Gray's Plain, the library was usually called Zoar.

Mrs. Bemis was a Scottish orphan who as a teenager had come to western Canada and eventually worked her way down to California at the time of the '49 gold rush. Frederick Bemis was a Newtown native who had come to the goldfields to make his fortune. Although he did not quite make a fortune, he did return to Newtown with a substantial amount of money and a wife. They settled at what is today the junction of High Rock Road. and Route 34. And that is where the library was located, in the Bemises' living room.

It is not known when the library was first opened, but Mrs. Bemis was a gregarious woman who enjoyed entertaining people in her home and used the library as a pretext for attracting visitors. She was only open formally on the first and second Sundays of each month, but she was known to lend books on other occasions especially to the district's children. A few days after the Boyd donation, she invited all of the district's children to come to her house on Saturday to assist in covering the new books. In this way she tended to the literary needs of that remote section of town.

Donations were not the only source of her books, however. She loved holding entertainments for the neighbors. The Bemises were the first in Newtown to buy an Edison cylinder phonograph and on the slightest pretext she would bring it out to play for all who wanted to hear her collection of recordings. Heavily represented among these were songs and spoken literature from her native Scotland. This was fondly remembered by Irving Wheeler Hall when he wrote his reminiscences of the Gray's Plain area a couple of decades ago.

Hall had lived with his Uncle Homer Clark between 1900 and 1911, at a time when his father was sick and his mother had trouble providing for her son. The Clark farm, which was called Arcadia for reasons no one seems to remember, was located on Route 34 directly across from Great Ring Road. From this location, young Hall, once his farm chores were completed, would wander across the landscape exploring. One of his favorite places to spend time was fishing in Warner Pond, which was owned by the Bemises. On his way home from one of these fishing expeditions, Mrs. Bemis invited him in to hear the new Edison machine. As he pointed out later, the Scottish songs sung by Harry Lauder that night changed his life. He learned to imitate the Scottish comic's style in song and patter and soon became relatively well known in the area for his performances. He later made a minor name for himself and once even had an opportunity to perform one of the Lauder standards for Lauder himself. It was natural that he would be one of the stars of the 1910 entertainment for the support of the library, which was favorably reviewed by *The Bee* and long remembered by the town.

The affair was held in the Morris' carriage house. This was located on the east side of Route 34, between the intersections of Zoar Road and Old Mill Road. The well-advertised event was held on Saturday, August 27. As *The Bee* described it, "The weather was perfect and by eight o'clock the roadway was lined with teams and automobiles and Mr. Morris' carriage house was literally crowded to overflowing." About 250 people were present, coming from all over eastern Newtown. The building had been modified to become a temporary theater. It was covered in bunting and flags and its walls were completely covered in red, white and blue with a solid red background for the stage. The stage was built of lumber that had been donated by Frederick Bemis among others and chairs had been borrowed from several Sandy Hook businesses including Ed Troy's hotel and Levi Morris' general store. The building was lighted with strings of Japanese lanterns and other chains of lanterns were hung along the approach to the carriage house all the way down to the road to light the way of the audience members.

The entertainment began sharply at 8:00 P.M. as Arthur Twining Hadley, then president of Yale who had married into the Morris family, presented a poetic Alphabet of Zoar that he felt was needed because Zoar had so increased in importance that it needed an alphabet of its own. He then read twenty-six stanzas that mentioned many of the neighbors and their foibles as well as features of the Zoar area which were gently made fun of to the delight, laughter, and applause of the audience. Appropriately, for "B:" "Mrs. Bemis, the library's founder, whatever is best on our bill centers round her." The rest of the strained rhymes and fractured meter served as a good prologue to the rest of the evening's fun.

Opening the musical portion of the program was Mrs. Bemis' Edison recording of Harry Lauder. The audience was then treated to the visual rendition of Lauder's material as Irving Hall in faux Scottish outfit danced and sang his way across the stage and back, accompanied by Charles G. Morris on the guitar. *The Bee* felt that Hall's performance was "even more than usually spirited and elicited rounds of applause." It was truly the highlight of the evening and Hall himself remembered it as one of the greatest triumphs of his early life, barring his performance in front of Lauder himself. The program then continued with seventeen more acts alternating with Hall's songs, phonograph recordings, recitations by several of the local culture mavens, an Irish sketch, and a "coon sketch" which is only described as hysterical and surely would have offended modern sensibilities.

The tangible results of the evening were $28.68 which would be used to purchase more books for Mrs. Bemis' library. But *The Bee* also noted that perhaps the best result of the evening was the neighborliness and good fellowship which it created. "It was the result of real cooperation, not of a few, but of many, and the size of the audience and its representative character, for it was gathered from localities as far distant as Zoar Bridge, Curtiss Hill [the middle of Riverside Road] and Newtown Street [Main Street], indicates in a gratifying way the cordial relations that exist amongst the dwellers among little communities bound together under the name of Newtown."

One other entertainment was held a year later in 1911, but this was performed in Glover Hall in Sandy Hook. The acts were similar, but without the artistry of Irving Hall who had left Newtown by then. In monetary terms the event was a greater success in that it realized forty-seven dollars, but this amount was not for books. It was added to a building fund bringing the total to $100 which led the supporters of the library to assume that they could soon begin building. A site measuring 50 X 100 ft. had already been donated on the corner of Gray's Plain Road and Route 34, next to the Gray's Plain school house. The reason for the building was space. The library at that time numbered 905 volumes and they occupied all of the wall space in Mrs. Bemis' living room. The aftermath of the second great entertainment was the great anticipation that the eastern part of Newtown would have a regional library with its own home.

Ironically, that is the last news story about the little library. The Bemises continued to live in their Gray's Plain house, presumably with the book collection, until Frederick died in 1924. Isabelle Bemis moved from the house and died a short time later in a Danbury nursing home. Hall vividly remembered seeing her for the last time a few days before her death, but he says nothing about her efforts to bring literacy to a corner of Newtown. The fate of the collection is completely unknown, and the Zoar Library remains an interesting footnote to the town's literary culture.

~ Chapter Four ~

The Cyrenius H. Booth Library

As the citizens of Newtown opened their copies of *The Newtown Bee*, on Friday May 30, 1930, they were treated to several surprises. The first was that the front page was almost completely taken up with the will of the recently deceased Mary Hawley. The will had been printed in its entirety. As the morbidly curious read down the provisions for her extraordinary wealth, one item must have especially caught the eye of anyone who was associated with the town's library. Miss Hawley had made a provision for the building of a new library and for an endowment fund, the interest from which would provide for operating and maintenance expenses on into the future:

> I give and bequeath to said town of Newtown the sum of $200,000 for the purpose of erecting and equipping a building to be used as a free public library and, if necessary, acquiring land for a site therefore in said town of Newtown, said library to be known as "The Cyrenius H. Booth Library" in memory of my grandfather, provision to be made in the said library for a historical room or rooms, said library to be open for public use at all reasonable times every afternoon and evening, including Sundays... I authorize my executors in the exercise of their discretion to cause to be placed in said historical rooms such of my antique furniture, furnishings and family portraits as to them shall seem fit and proper and to take such steps as in their discretion may be necessary to have same kept therein permanently.

In the next paragraph she included a provision for $250,000 to be held by a Hartford bank in trust as the "Cyrenius H. Booth Fund." The yearly income from these invested funds was then to be used for the maintenance, support, and upkeep of the library, including the purchase of books and supplies. By this provision, Hawley had avoided all of the problems faced by the town's predecessor libraries as they struggled to raise funds to keep a current collection of books.

And thus, with two paragraphs, the Cyrenius H. Booth Library was created.

Mary Elizabeth Hawley and Cyrenius H. Booth

After the scandal of her disastrous marriage, Mary Hawley retreated into becoming nearly a complete recluse. Much of this was due to her overbearing mother who had been implicated in the collapse of her daughter's marriage. Stories abound of the miserly lifestyle that she adopted with her daughter, especially after the mitigating hand of Marcus was removed with his death. At the time that Sarah Hawley lay in her final illness in 1920, her doctor had to insist that she install a phone, even though phone service had been available in Newtown since the 1880s and she was one of the wealthiest women in the county.

With her mother's death, Mary Hawley flourished. She did not become a partying socialite but she did show signs of enjoying the life her wealth could afford. She kept her horses but also bought two Pierce Arrow automobiles and hired a man to tend to the driving and their maintenance. She traveled to Canada to see her relatives and made many trips to the rose garden in Hartford's Elizabeth Park, which stimulated the development of her own gardens, turning them into a Main Street showplace. She also began to take an active interest in the formation of the Hawley Family Society in 1923 and attended its annual meetings. But the most dramatic change in her life came as a result of the fire alarm that was spread by the telephone exchange at 11:30 on the evening of June 19, 1920.

The high school was on fire and the entire upper floor would soon be gutted and destroyed. The old building had been constructed to house the Newtown Academy and had originally stood on the summit of Sunset Hill. The old academy did not prosper and it was felt that the location was to blame, so in 1892 it was moved on rollers across the fields at the base of the hill, across the Boulevard and onto a foundation located just across Church Hill Road from St. Rose Church. It still did not prosper and in 1902 the town first rented and then bought the building to be used as the town's first high school.

By 1919 the high school had run into factional problems. At the beginning of that year, with the dismissal of a very popular teacher and the sympathetic resignation of two others, there was a split in the community that led to the creation of another competing high school known as the Community School. This was the situation at the time of the fire, and accusations concerning the cause of the fire were flung by each faction at each other, even though the cause was never discovered.

At this point Arthur T. Nettleton, the controlling officer of the Newtown Savings Bank and a friend and financial advisor to Mary Hawley, approached her with a proposition. She had money and she was essentially heirless. Therefore she was in a position to donate money to build a new school, which might bring the feuding factions back into harmony. She almost immediately began to work with an architect to design the most modern high school building possible, and presented the plans to the town along with the $100,000 necessary to build it. In 1925 she added another $100,000 to be put into a trust fund for the maintenance of the building, so the new high school would not cost the taxpayers of Newtown anything, even in the future. This proposal was accepted and the Hawley School, named after her parents, was built. The social chasm was also healed.

Philanthropy became her. Now that she had the feel for spending money on public projects, others followed. In 1924 she arranged for the entrance of the Village Cemetery to be entirely re-landscaped. Entrance gates were built and plantings were arranged around the circular driveway that led around to the new holding vault that she had constructed. The roadway leading up to the entrance, now fittingly called Hawley Lane, was rebuilt and a bridge was built over the spillway of the pond she had created at the southern end of the Ram Pasture.

Mary Elizabeth Hawley

While all of this was happening, she was also busily involved in buying up pieces of real estate in the village including the abandoned Newtown Inn and the lot on which it stood. Some felt that she had purchased this to keep it from reopening since it had a once-notorious bar room on the ground floor. Her real reason was a well-hidden secret for the next six years.

The next major benefaction was the Edmond Town Hall. In June 1928, Hawley, through Arthur T. Nettleton, approached the town with an offer of $250,000 to build a new town hall, along with $100,000 which was to be put into a trust fund for the building's maintenance. As with the Hawley School, she stipulated that the building be named for one of her relatives, this time, Judge William Edmond, her maternal great grandfather. Quickly a building committee was convened under the leadership of Nettleton and the architect Philip Sunderland of Danbury was hired to draw up the plans.

Ground was broken late in 1928 and by May 1, 1929, there was enough of the building constructed to hold a cornerstone ceremony. This was the only public appearance that Mary Hawley ever made. She stepped up to the cornerstone, which was dangling at the end of a derrick cable over the place it was to be set and with a trowel handed to her by one of the masons, set a trowelful of cement beneath the stone. More cement was added by the mason, smoothed off, and the stone was lowered to the applause of over 100 people who had gathered to witness the event.

The cornerstone laying was also her last public appearance. She was sick with congestive heart failure and advanced arteriosclerosis. As the building was rushed to completion, it was a frequently expressed hope that she would live to see its completion. That was not to be, for at 8:05 P.M. on Sunday May 11, 1930, she died. The building would not be open to the public until August 22, but the bell in the town hall cupola tolled for the first time as her funeral cortege proceeded down Main Street to the holding vault she had donated six years before.

Her will held the surprise of two more benefactions: a monument for Newtown's war dead and the library, which according to the tradition she had established, was to be named for a member of her family, this time her maternal grandfather, Cyrenius H. Booth. Unlike Judge Edmond who was fairly well-remembered, Dr. Booth would need to be reintroduced to the town in which he had practiced.

Cyrenius H. Booth

Booth was a descendent of one of Newtown's pioneering families and, according to Ezra Johnson, Newtown's first unofficial historian, he was "a doctor of the old school." He was born on May 25, 1797, and he acquired his medical knowledge in the typical fashion of the time by apprenticing under Dr. Bennett Perry, Newtown's leading eighteenth century physician. Booth also attended a long series of lectures on medicine delivered by Dr. Hosack of New York who was considered a leading physician of his time. In this he was anticipating the modern medical training of late nineteenth and early twentieth centuries. As a doctor, he truly had one foot in the eighteenth and one in the nineteenth century.

On October 1, 1820, Dr. Booth married Sarah Edmond, the daughter of Judge William Edmond, and that same year he built a small three-bay house on the east side of Main Street, just two doors south of where the modern library would be situated. Here he set up housekeeping and conducted his practice of medicine until his death in 1871. Sarah and Cyrenius had three children: William, who went on in medicine becoming a dentist in Danbury until his death in 1859 at the age of 37; Mary, who married Henry Sanford, one of Newtown's most successful merchants; and Sarah, who married Marcus Hawley and became the mother of Mary Elizabeth.

After her father's death, Sarah, who ruled the domestic scene tightly, convinced Marcus to move to Newtown from Bridgeport where they had been living and where Mary had been born. The railroad made this move possible for him. Since he was a major stockholder in the Housatonic Railroad, he could easily commute to his offices in Bridgeport and New York on a daily basis and leave Sarah to enjoy the return to her childhood home. Before the move, however, she had the old house completely renovated and enlarged to almost twice its original square footage. Recently when this building was being renovated to become the Inn at Newtown, the remains of Dr. Booth's original house were discovered in the walls. Sarah had not torn down the old house but had built around it encapsulating it in her new home.

By all accounts, Cyrenius H. Booth was a well-respected man. Ezra Johnson remembered him and commented, "For half a century practically, the doctor was a familiar figure, driving over hills and along the valleys in answer to the beck and call of its town's people, his saddle bags filled with pills and nostrums for ills to which the flesh is heir. The writer remembers him as a man of infinite mirth, a famous story teller and a great favorite with children and young people." He was a typical country doctor of the time whose immortality is due solely to his granddaughter.

Building A Model Library

When the excitement of the discovery that Newtown was to have a new up-to-date library abated somewhat, the Cyrenius H. Booth Library Committee was formed to get the project started. Its first meeting was held in the newly completed Edmond Town Hall on December 9, 1930, and consisted of Thomas F. Brew, a respected local building contractor who would officially head the committee, Sanford Mead, Thomas Holian, Rodney Shepard, who was the partner of Levi Morris in the General Store, Charles G. Morris, a noted lawyer, and Herbert C. Hubbell, who was effectively second-in-command at the Newtown Savings Bank. Arthur T. Nettleton did not officially appear as part of this committee, but he was heavily involved in the early planning and became the head of the Board of Trustees when it was finally formed the next year.

The C.H. Booth Library as it looked in 1932

Its first task was to pick an architect. That was quickly accomplished since the town's experience with Philip Sunderland on the Edmond Town Hall and even earlier on the Hawley School, had been so positive. He was contracted with on January 2, 1931, to design the library as well. By April 30, the committee was ready to approve in substance the plans that Sunderland had drawn up and by July 16, the final plans were approved after several minor revisions.

Before construction could begin another problem had to be solved: where to put the building. Consulting Arthur Nettleton it was discovered that Miss Hawley had purchased the old Newtown Inn in 1925, anticipating that the library would go on that plot of ground. She, however, neglected to put this into her will and the rest, residue, and remainder of her estate, after all of the other distributions were made, went to Yale, so Yale University owned the Newtown Inn. Negotiations went well since Yale had no desire to be a Newtown landlord and the property was deeded to the town along with the Ram Pasture. Now the process of building a library could continue. On September 15 the bids were opened and contracts were awarded for the general contractor, plumbing, heating and electrical work.

Sunderland had planned the building to include all of the latest and most modern library features. The core of the library was the two stack rooms, one on the main floor and the other in the basement, connected by a central enclosed staircase and capable of holding up to 25,000 volumes. But more important was the overall atmosphere of the new building. It was to be homey and inviting, so he designed it as a brick Georgian residence, avoiding the institutional look of so many other libraries of the time. The commodious reading rooms had fireplaces against each outside wall with painted portraits of the library's namesake and his wife over the mantel. They were furnished with comfortable overstuffed chairs and sofas which were made-to-order by the Erskine-Danforth Company of Stamford. That company was also responsible for the design and execution of the lighting fixtures and the window treatment on the first floor. The main public rooms were also finished with an attention to detail that is rare in any public building. The neo-classical ceiling molding had been milled especially for the library, and are still evident in the library's original rooms as is the wooden wainscoting running around the walls except where the placement of bookcases in modern times has obscured it.

In addition, there was attention given to the practical nature of a library. The building was fireproof and all of the public rooms were treated with Acousti-Celatex ceiling tiles and cork floors to deaden the sound. A Doherty-Brehn humidifying system was set up in the basement so that properly conditioned air could be ducted to every room. To make maintenance of the building easier, it had the latest Spencer Turbine central vacuum cleaning system in the basement with pipe outlets in every room. The custodian only had to carry around a short section of vacuum hose which could be plugged into a convenient baseboard outlet rather than lug a heavy machine from room to room and floor to floor.

In the basement was a meeting room that was appointed in the same comfortable manner as the reading rooms and capable of accommodating up to 100 people. Three of its walls were paneled from floor to ceiling with pine boards of varying widths. Along the south wall was a fireplace imitating those in the reading rooms. The floors of the room and the foyer were paved in flagstone which was rough in texture and laid in the manner of the cathedrals of England. This room also had a separate hall and entrance so meetings could be conducted after the library itself had closed.

The library's reading room located to the right of the main entrance as it appeared in 1932

The second story had three exhibition galleries for the library's historical collections, which at first consisted of a large number of antiques that Mary Hawley had inherited from her many Newtown ancestors. The north and south gallery also had fireplaces and they were furnished with a selection of eighteenth and nineteenth century chairs, several of which were made in Newtown or the surrounding area. A series of flat and standing cases, which had been specially made for the library, were placed strategically around the room. In these, delicate artifacts could be safely displayed. The central gallery contained formal portraits for Mary Hawley and her family. Together these rooms formed a local history museum of a type that is still frequently seen in small English villages.

A reading room located to the left of the main entrance as it appeared in 1932. It now serves as the Local History and Genealogy Room

To fulfill the provisions of her will, a suite of historical rooms extended to the rear of the building from a landing halfway up the colonial staircase that greeted patrons as they entered the building. Here was displayed Hawley's heirloom dining room furniture along with two built-in corner cupboards that exhibited her old lusterware. The walls were decorated with a rare copy of an old French hand-block scenic wallpaper. To the north of the dining room was a smaller bedroom that contained Hawley's antique four-poster bed and sundry other pieces of her bedroom furniture. Both of these rooms were floored with wide oak boards.

The Mary Hawley dining room displaying her furniture. The corner would later be opened for a door allowing a second means of egress from the second floor galleries. Beyond this the room has been preserved as it was when first opened to the public.

Mary Hawley's bedroom furniture. The room displaying her furniture remained intact until the failure of the first addition attempt when the room was converted into a foyer for the north gallery hall. The furniture was reassembled in the fore-attic where it can be seen today very much as it appears here.

On Saturday December 17, 1932, the building was ready and opened to the public for the first time.

The Structure of a New Library

With the new building well underway, attention turned to the structure and personnel who would make the library function. Fundamental to this was the Board of Trustees who met for the first time in the Edmond Town Hall on September 1, 1931. Twenty-four of Newtown's leading citizens comprised this first board and their first order of business was to vote Arthur T. Nettleton to be their chairman and Herbert C. Hubbell as clerk. This being done, Nettleton led them to elect the first officers of the corporation who were Nettleton, president; Charles G. Morris, vice president; Alice Carroll, secretary, and Rodney P. Shepard, treasurer. Alice Carroll was to become the longest serving member of the board, only resigning in 1987 due to poor health. Forty-five of those fifty-seven years of service were as secretary.

Alice Carroll

Arthur T. Nettleton's role in the formation of the library was vital, as it had been in the other benefactions of Mary Hawley. He served for seventeen years as president and dominated the meetings, guiding the formation of policy and molding the very nature of the library. A quiet and unassuming man, his role in the shaping of twentieth century Newtown is little known. He was the guiding force behind the Newtown Savings Bank for over fifty years and he insured that the bank remained the center of the town's economic infrastructure and that its staff remained deeply involved in the community, a tradition which lives on in the current bank's management. He served on the building committees of the Hawley School and the Edmond Town Hall and strongly influenced that of the new library. This insured the finest quality of design and planning for these buildings. He not only guided the creation of the building but, through either his presence or influence on their governing boards, he also guided the direction that these institutions took.

Nettleton was an austere and dominant man, precise to a fault and of the greatest integrity. He was also benevolent, frequently taking young high school students into the bank, giving them after-school employment. This often led to promotion and in a couple of cases to a career in banking. A widely kept secret that only came out as part of a eulogy after his death in 1951 was that he yearly picked a promising young student and paid for his college education. This was the man who would mold the library into a social, educational, and cultural center of Newtown over the next seventeen years.

By late December 1931, the rest of the vital personnel were hired although they would not begin work until December 1, 1932. Chief among these was the first head librarian, William N. Strong, and the first assistant librarian, Vera Tracy. For Strong the position was the beginning of a second career. He had come originally from northeastern Pennsylvania and had graduated with honors from Colgate University. He taught Greek and English for two years before returning to graduate school at Colgate and then the State College for teachers in Albany. At the turn of the century he began a twenty-five-year teaching career in the New York school system eventually serving as a high school principal.

In 1927, he moved to Newtown and, after his notification of being hired as librarian, he began an intensive course of study in library services at Columbia. Even though his salary did not begin until December 1, he spent the year before that touring other libraries to learn their procedures. He also consulted with the library building committee regarding equipment and other details, and was responsible for purchasing and preparing 4,000 books as a basis of the new collection. Because the building was not yet ready, most of this work was done in the new town hall and then transferred to the new library's stacks shortly before opening.

Clearly Strong was a scholar, well educated, and academic, every quality that should make a strong library administrator. It came as a great surprise therefore, when at the first annual meeting in September 1933, the position of head librarian went to Vera Tracy by a vote of 14 to 8, thus effectively firing Strong. He was stunned. He had assumed the position was to be a long term one and in a letter to *The Bee* he complained of the way in which he had been fired, hearing about it from one of the trustees who had supported him, without any warning of his impending dismissal. The reasons for passing the position to Miss Tracy are not clear. His letter was never answered or, if it was, it had been as a private letter which has not survived. *The Bee* is also mysteriously silent, but knowing the policy of the editors of that paper to not cover scandal, they may have simply chosen to not cover the issue. The vote tallies strongly suggest some political motivations on the part of the trustees, but at this distance in time the reasons for his dismissal will never be known. Regardless of the reason, Vera Tracy, would be the library's first effective librarian and would successfully administer the new library for the next six years.

The Historical Collections

An important facet of the early library and one that has become almost completely forgotten by its modern patrons was the historical collections. At the same meeting which dismissed Librarian Strong, Herbert C. Hubbell was voted to be the head of the historical collections. At first this position was to determine how best to display the antiques from the Mary Hawley estate.

This was done in the two historical rooms, but there was a large quantity of other antiques and family memorabilia that had come to the library with the dining room and bedroom furniture. Much of this was put into some of the flat cases; the family papers were stored, but not cataloged in the basement vault. Many years later they would provide remarkable insight into Hawley and her ancestors to Newtown's first official historian.

At the same meeting Hubbell was also put in charge of another large collection of Newtown memorabilia donated by Arthur Nettleton. This collection had come from the estate of Charles Henry Peck. Peck had been the town clerk for a decade in the late nineteenth century and so had developed a passion for the town and its history. As a project with his son, he began to collect relics and some documents of the town's past. As his interest became more widely known, many of the town's older families began to donate family memorabilia to his growing museum. A museum it actually became as he fitted the front room of the Balcony House (34 Main Street) in which he lived, with shelves and display cases and crammed them with the town's jetsam.

Tragically, Peck's son died in his early teenage years. Peck continued to collect town relics as a tribute to his son, but his heart was no longer in the collection. When Arthur Nettleton came to Newtown looking for a place to live while he began his short-lived career as a merchant, Peck and his wife took him in. Since Nettleton was about the same age as Peck's son, an unusually strong bond developed between them and they effectively adopted him. When Hannah Peck died in the 1920s, Nettleton inherited the house and its collections. These documents and relics, which were to be formally known as the Charles H. Peck Collection, were what Nettleton donated on that night in September 1933.

In June of the next year, the collections of the now defunct John Beach Memorial Library were formally accepted by the Board of Trustees. This collection consisted of books and memorial funds, but it also included a number of historical artifacts that had been given to the Beach Library, such as Sanford's sword, a collection of *Middlebrook's Almanacs* 1852-1900, and a bound collection of *The Connecticut Journal* 1789-1791. A spectacular addition to the collection was a surveyor's compass and chain which had been given to the Beach Library by T. W. Glover. According to his notation, this equipment had been used throughout the eighteenth century to survey the land layout and roads for over half of the town.

These collections became the foundation for the library's outstanding displays of historical artifacts which transformed the upper galleries into a local history museum. Although those galleries have not remained as display areas, the library's still-impressive collections are displayed on a rotating basis throughout the library in the same display cases that were specially built to hold them. The position of head of historical collections slowly died out in the trustees' minute book, but it was resurrected in 1982 when Caroline Stokes was voted to fill the newly created position of curator of the library's collections. Under her guidance the pieces in the collections have been identified and labeled, and a precession of displays have been mounted so that the original intention of Mary Hawley and the early trustees has been recognized and continued.

~ *Chapter Five* ~

The Middle Years

By the end of the 1930s, the Cyrenius H. Booth Library had been fully established and a routine was in place that would guide the library relatively unchanged until the early 1980s. The number of cardholders had increased rapidly until 1939 when Miss Tracy reported that there were 1,670 which represented sixty-five and a half percent of the town's population.

The main hall and check-out desk as it looked the day the C.H. Booth Library opened in 1932

The collection had also more than doubled to 13,000 from what it had been when the library opened. This was the state of the library when Vera Tracy resigned in February of 1939 to accept the position of head librarian in West Hartford. Her replacement found the need to implement several reforms but the library would not change radically through the tenure of the next five librarians.

Alice P. Hancock: The Well Qualified Professional

Alice Hancock was born and educated in Baltimore Maryland. Her college experience began at the University of Montana where she earned an A.B. and M.A. and then stayed on to teach English for three years. The library was her first love however, so she started a degree in library science at the University of Wisconsin and finished it at the Columbia University School of Library Science. This assured her a position with the New York City Library where she spent four years, first in reference and then in the children's department. When she applied for the position in Newtown she was on a leave of absence to work in the State Library of Albany where she was one of three people who reviewed new books and prepared syllabi for other librarians in the state.

Alice Hancock Davidson

Miss Hancock was one of the best qualified of the library's early librarians. It was therefore natural that, after a couple of months learning the existing procedures, she would see the need for some professional reforms. Accordingly, she delivered a report to the board that contained the following three recommendations: 1) Move the book collection, which had been crowded into one stack area into the other stack shelves; 2) Discard worn and outdated books, and 3) Begin the process of taking inventory, something which had not been done since the library opened. Regarding the strange recommendation to move the book collection she explained:

> When I came to the library June 1st I found that the adult collection of books was crowded into one section of the stacks. Since there was not nearly enough room for all of the books in so small a space this meant that books were piled on top of each other or wedged so tightly on the shelves that it was difficult to remove them. While there was this congestion in one half of the stacks, the other half, except for a section of books waiting to be examined and discarded, was entirely empty.

After this was done she tackled the process of inventory and weeding the collection. The inventory was on-going and by September 1940 she had winnowed the collection to 13,466, discarding 526 books, many of which had come from the old Beach Library.

In 1941 Marguerite Raynolds began her forty-one-year association with the library. She became a trustee in July, joining her husband, Robert, a well-known local author, who was one of the early trustees. Marguerite's special interest was always the school, and that interest began, as it does for so many mothers, with her own children. Reminiscing in the late 1980s, she explained that her children's teacher asked if she helped them with their homework because they seemed to have such a strong background. She told the teacher she did not help them, but that she did bring them books from the library that seemed to relate to what they were doing in school. The teacher then asked her if she would bring books to the classroom for the other children that she was teaching and Marguerite agreed. By the end of the year taking books to the classroom had become established as a regular part of the library routine and the circulation of children's fiction doubled to 4,462 and non-fiction to 505. As a result of her efforts she was eventually offered $3,000 to become the first librarian at the Hawley School, although she was asked by her husband to not accept the stipend as it would be discouraging for him to have his wife earning more money than he did.

In 1941 the library was also beginning to feel anticipation of the war that would be declared in December. In her annual report, Miss Hancock noted that although there was a noticeable increase in juvenile circulation, there was a dramatic drop in adult numbers. This drop she attributed to, "…the world situation in general and especially to the development of the defense industry, to war work, and to conscription. Many people who were formerly steady readers are now so occupied that their leisure is greatly curtailed." This effect would be felt even more keenly after the bombing of Pearl Harbor.

The Library at War

In March of 1942 Miss Hancock became Mrs. Davidson and, by the time of the annual report for her first year as a married woman, she noted that there was a further decline in library patronage. Her analysis of the situation is an insightful glimpse into the home front in Newtown during the war. "People throughout the country, faced with new duties in the war effort, have less time for reading. The gasoline shortage has also had a noticeable effect on our book circulation. Many people from the outlying districts who formally drove to the library two or three times a week cannot afford to use gasoline to do so." There was nothing she could do to alleviate the gas shortages, but she felt that the library could become more convenient to the public by being open in the morning. She therefore recommended the library schedule be extended to Tuesday mornings from 10:00 A.M. to noon.

Davidson also reasoned that the problem of traveling to get books during the gas rationing could be partially solved by making the Sandy Hook Library more available. Previously, this library was only open for short periods of time one afternoon a week and on Saturday depending on the availability of the volunteer librarian. The staff of the Booth Library, working with the board of the Sandy Hook Library, arranged to open every Thursday afternoon for the circulation of books and for a children's story hour. In her analysis of this effort at the end of the year she noted that there was no response by adults to this extension of hours, but there was a great response by children and their participation in the story hours was, "... unfailing and increasing."

As the war deepened the effects on the library became more dramatic. By early 1943, in order to save rationed fuel oil, it was voted to close the library on Sundays, regardless of the provision in the Hawley will to be open seven days a week. Davidson's report for the annual meeting, following this decision reflects the home front during the depth of the war in such a compelling way that it is worth repeating in its entirety:

> There were ...the seemingly endless winter months when the fuel oil gave out and a new supply was unobtainable. So we moved into the children's room behind newly installed doors, borrowed electric heaters from the Thrift Shop and generous neighbors, and with those, the fireplaces, and layers of sweaters managed to carry on in a temperature rarely above sixty degrees and at times as low as forty-eight. A trip to the stacks, which we dubbed "The refrigerating plant," was done in double quick time and brought us shivering back to the fireplace. Evening work was impossible, and from December to mid-May the library closed at six P.M. Club work for the children had to be abandoned for we had no warm place for them to meet. The OPA[2] clamped down on bus transportation and from

---

[2] Office of Price Administration.

Christmas until spring no more school classes could be brought to the library for weekly story hours. Like pioneers we piled wood on the fire and dug in for the winter.

During the vacation period all aspiring young soldiers joined the Book Brigade, a summer reading club. Starting in as buck privates they rose, according to the number of books read and reported, to non-commissioned and then commissioned officers. When the club was disbanded late in August we had no less than one general, one brigadier general, a good sprinkling of colonels, majors and captains. There was not a private left to take orders from the few poor sergeants.

Because of gasoline rationing, and particularly after the ban was placed on pleasure driving, people in the outlying districts found it almost impossible to come to the library. Until this year book circulation during the summer months has always increased and July and August have been our busiest time. This summer day after day went by with only a handful of people coming in. New books as well as old stood unread on the shelves. And yet many people had more time for reading than ever before. Again and again plaintive voices over the phone asked to have long overdue books to be renewed once again. Clearly something had to be done about it; clearly, too, one car taking the library to the people would require far less gas than thirty or forty cars bringing people to the library. My car stood idle in the garage week after week and the carrier would hold one or two hundred books, the back seat a good hundred more. Why not use it for a bookmobile? It was certainly worth the experiment. Mr. Smith at the rationing board granted us a gasoline allotment. Mr. Stoddard devised a makeshift book carrier from cardboard cartons; Mrs Mitchell and I selected a small library of books - adult and juvenile, fiction and non-fiction, new and old. Then at 9:00 A.M. on June 30 we started off. Our equipment aside from books was a small box containing a stamp pad and daters and an old fashioned school bell with which to announce our arrival. That first morning we drove only through Taunton and Dodgingtown districts and by noon we had circulated forty-five books. A few houses were closed, a few people were "too busy to read," but the majority were grateful and enthusiastic. They were hungry for books and until we came along had no means of getting them. Children came scampering at the sound of the bell and clambered eagerly into the back seat where the juvenile books were arranged. Their mothers left the garden or kitchen to pore (sic) over our wares and went away arms laden. One woman was only a voice high up in a cherry tree. Yes, she'd love something but she couldn't get down until the fire department came with a ladder. We left books on a nearby stone wall and promised to look for her again in two weeks, either at her home or at the hospital. Another woman we discovered under a tree by the roadside, sitting under a hat, I might say, for here like the Quangle Wangle Queen's in Lear's poem seemed just about "a hundred and two feet wide." She was waiting for the milkman; a book was just what she wanted. She would be in the same place at the same time two weeks later, and if we were not there at the appointed hour she'd just sit on indefinitely until we appeared.

Mrs. Davidson's qualifications were such that she was recruited to help the war effort by becoming the librarian for the War Department. She was granted a one-year leave of absence in September of 1943, but this was extended twice as the war dragged on. She finally returned to her Booth Library post on June 1, 1945. Her husband, however, continued to live in Washington and within a year she began to find the separation very difficult. In her letter of resignation she explained that both she and her husband had hoped to settle permanently in Newtown after the war but that had proved unfeasible, so she left to join him in January of 1946.

During Davidson's leave of absence, Sarah Mitchell, who had been serving as assistant librarian since 1933, filled in as acting head librarian. Mitchell's association with the Newtown libraries was long standing. She had been born in Newtown in 1897 and had attended school in the Palestine one-room schoolhouse. Her first connection with library work came when she joined the finance committee of the John Beach Library in 1926. When the Booth Library was under construction in 1931, she had volunteered to worked in the temporary quarters in Edmond Town Hall preparing books for the move into the new building. It is not surprising therefore that she became the assistant librarian once it opened. She would serve as acting head librarian several more times before finally becoming head librarian in her own right.

The Post War Library

After Davidson's resignation, Sarah Mitchell again served as acting head librarian while the search committee sought another "trained librarian." The emphasis was on "trained" which was repeated at least twice in the charge to the search committee. Unfortunately Mitchell was not a trained librarian, but Gladys B. Dexter was and she became the new head librarian in July of 1946. She had received an advanced degree from Boston University's School of Religious Education and from Simmons College in Library Science. She then gained library experience as a cataloger and assistant librarian in Chelsea, Massachusetts, while doing editorial work for the American Imprint Society. For the previous three years she had been the librarian at Endicott Junior College in Beverly, Massachusetts.

Gladys Dexter

Here was a trained librarian, but Newtown was apparently not ready to do what was necessary to keep her and her stay here was short. On September 8, 1948, Arthur Nettleton read her letter of resignation to the board in which she claimed that her resignation was made "… in view of the apparent impossibility of …securing annual increments and a maximum salary comparable with the levels of salaries now being paid. It is to be regretted that in order to further my professional advancement, this action is necessary." The board accepted her resignation and again voted for Sarah Mitchell to be acting head librarian until 1951 when another librarian with professional training could be hired.

Meanwhile, as the war ended, the library labored to return to operating in a post-war world. By May 5, 1945, even before the war was completely over, the library resumed Sunday hours, bringing it back into compliance with the Hawley will. Davidson's bookmobile was discontinued. Gas may have again been plentiful, but post-war economic conditions dictated cutbacks elsewhere in library operations. Within the year, Sunday hours were again eliminated, and the normal library hours on weekdays were cut to just afternoons from 1:00 to 6:00. Saturdays the hours remained 10:00 A.M. to 6:00 P.M. to serve patrons on a day that most had free from work.

The Cyrenius H. Booth Library, Newtown, Conn.

The C.H. Booth Library in 1945 at the end of W.W. II

In 1948 Raymond Fosdick headed a committee to review the library's financial standing. Up to this point the library had been completely self sustaining with the income that was generated by the Hawley Trust Fund. After the war, that income became strained as the library began to expand its collections and services, requiring additional personnel. The results of the Fosdick committee was a resolution that, "The board authorize and appeal to the residents and friends of Newtown to contribute to a special fund to help maintain and improve the services of the Newtown Library." This was the first time that the new library issued a public appeal for personal contributions. It would hardly be the last. By the last two decades of the twentieth century, this type of fund-raising would become an annual event.

The year 1948 marked another milestone for the library. Arthur T. Nettleton, the guiding light of the library's creation, and its first and only president, was again elected president of the board for the coming year. But immediately after the election, he presented his resignation effective by the next quarterly meeting in December. It was accepted with regret and he was voted member emetitus of the board, which was the first time that this status was bestowed. Nettleton was slowing down.

For the previous decade he had been suffering from arteriosclerosis, but he had perservered in his duties at the bank and his other community interests. Now, however, he was forced to cut back on those other obligations. There was one further glorious moment in his life when he was asked to give a short speech, something he never did normally, at the dedication of the new steel flagpole on Lincoln's birthday in 1950. Nettleton had been the motivational force behind making the flagpole in the middle of Main Street a permanent landmark. The strain of the public event created debilitating pain that led him to enter the hospital. Once there he realized that he could no longer even carry out the duties of treasurer and president of the Newtown Savings Bank which he had so successfully pursued for the previous fifty years, and so submitted his resignation, which was only accepted with deep regret by the bank board. Nettleton languished at Danbury Hospital until August 12, 1951, when a cerebral thrombosis, a blood clot on the brain, ended his life. A month before his death, a new trained librarian assumed her duties at the library.

Mary Lucas was even more well-trained than her predecessor had been. She was a native of Pennsylvania and had attended Carnegie Library School, received an A.B. degree from Waynesburg College and a master's from the Graduate Library School of the University of Chicago. Her job experience was extensive. She had served as librarian in the Lower East Side Branch of the New York Public Library and had been head librarian for the main libraries in Duluth, Minnesota, Atlanta, Georgia, Providence, Rhode Island, and Newark, New Jersey, from which she came to take over active duty in Newtown on July 9, 1951. She had also taught at the Library School of Columbia and was the author of *Organization and Administration of Library Services for Children*.

Mary Lucas

As is to be expected from the title of her book, one of Librarian Lucas' priorities at the Booth Library was its children's programs. Surprisingly, in the her annual report of 1954 she noted that there was a drop in juvenile circulation for the second year in a row. The cause of the drop, she felt, was partially due to the increasing popularity of television, making this one of the earliest observations on technology's negative impact on a public institution such as the library. This was not the only cause, for she goes on to note, "... There are few children within walking distance of the library; families are becoming increasingly reluctant to have children ride their bicycles to the library, because of increasing traffic, so they, the parents, must bring children in many cases - sometimes it is the father after dinner." There is undoubtly no connection, but on July 6 of the next year, Lucas submitted her resignation. With thirty-six years of library work, she was ready to retire after serving Newtown for four years. This time the board did not form a search committee to look for another "well-trained librarian." They already had one. Immediately after voting to accept Lucas' resignation, it was voted to make Sarah Mitchell head librarian at a salary of $3,200.

The Julia Brush Collection

The decades of the 1950s and 1960s were relatively quiet ones for the library, but there were two bequests that would give the library special research capabilities in two different areas: genealogy and art. The first was the unique personal collection of genealogies and local histories owned by a noted local genealogist Julia Brush.

Julia Brush

Brush had been born in Hawleyville in 1862 as one of four children of Robert and Emeline Clark. When a young child, her mother contracted a serious illness and Julia was taken in by her aunt and uncle on their farm on Stony Hill, where she grew up. She married Chester H. Brush, who was in charge of Indian Affairs under both Theodore Roosevelt and William Howard Taft, and so she lived much of her early family life in Washington, D.C. While there she developed a deep interest in genealogy and began collecting reference books, concentrating on Connecticut families.

After her husband's death she moved back to Connecticut, settling in Danbury, where she continued to develop her interest in family histories and to add them to her library. It was also during this period that she became active in the Daughters of the American Revolution and was instrumental in helping many local women qualify for the DAR by tracing their ancestry back to a Revolutonary War patriot. By the time of her death on October 28, 1942, she had developed a substantial reputation and a library of over 1,000 specialized books.

The Brush house and library were inherited by her daughter, Mrs. David Bliss, but a provision in her will stipulated that the library was to be given intact to a local public library. There were rumors that it had been offered first to the Danbury Public Library but they turned it down as too specialized for their patrons' interests. The next logical choice was the library in her natal town, and the board formally accepted the bequest during its quarterly meeting on June 3, 1953.

The collection was received a few months later after which Mary Lucas and her staff set to work cataloging the books and integrating it with the other genealogical volumes that the library already owned. While this was being done, a set of shelves was built running around the second floor mezzanine to hold the collection. (The collection remained there until the first expansion in the 1980s when it was stuffed into the old staff lounge in the basement. After the next expansion in the late 1990s, it was moved to the first-floor front room.) With the collection in place and ready to serve the public, a reception was held on November 7, 1954, to celebrate what President Fosdick characterized as an "outstanding small collection."

As the librarians worked through the Julia Brush Collection it rapidly became apparent how outstanding and extraordinary it was. In addition to many rare genealogies of local families and some equally rare histories of many Connecticut towns, there was a complete bound set of the *New England Historical and Geneaological Register* going back to the first issue of 1847. There was also a complete set of the DAR Lineage books going back to the first issue in 1891. Even rarer was a complete bound set of *The New York Genealogical and Biographical Record* beginning in 1869, and the complete *Families of Ancient New Haven* (later to become the *American Geneaologist*) begun by the noted genealogist, Donald Lines Jacobus. Due to the foresight of Lucas and her successors, subscription to these publications have been continued down to the present. They have also added new town histories and family genealogies as they became available so that today it is the best genealogical and local history facility in the western part of the state and a mecca for those doing research on local families.

John Angel and the Library's Magnificent Art Collection

Six years after the Julia Brush reception, the board received news that it was to be the recipient of a substantial collection of art books that had belonged to the internationally renowned sculptor, John Angel. Angel had been born, brought up, and educated in Devonshire, England near Exeter. As a boy he had wandered through the cathedral at Exeter and was so enchanted by what he saw that he made a career choice as a sculptor. After years of study at the Albert Memorial and Lambeth Art Schools in London, he became a student at the Royal Academy school where he was awarded the first of many silver medals for his work. Between 1917 and 1927 he exhibited regularly at the Royal Academy and the accolades won there led to commissions for World War I memorials in Exeter, Rotherdam, and Bridgewater. The Exeter memorial, which was dedicated in the early 1920s, brought him national and then international attention. By 1927, he had received an invitation to come to the United States to execute the Gothic sculpture for the Cathedral Church of St. John the Divine in New York. He would go on to do the bronze doors at St. Patrick's Cathedral in New York, sculpture for the Princeton University chapel and for the National Shrine of the Immaculate Conception in Washington, D.C. He also executed the commission for the heroic statues of the four evangelists for the Cathedral of St. Paul in St. Paul, Minnesota.

In 1940 Angel moved to Sandy Hook. The old mill at the dam of Warner's pond (on Old Mill Road.) had been converted into a house and he bought this, immediately adding a studio. He later built another new studio near the old one that had been specially reinforced to stand the multi-ton weight of the heroic sculptures he worked on. It was here that he produced most of the pieces for the ecclesiastical building mention above. Here he spent the rest of his life, dying on October 16, 1960, at the age of 78.

In April of the following year, Angel's sons Laurence and Henry presented their father's art books to the library. By December of 1962, the collection had been cataloged and placed in special book cases made by Edward Wright in the upstairs south gallery. Angel's sons also donated several plaster casts done as studies for Angel's work and photographs of him working in his studio. Wright built a pedestal for the plaster model of Alexander Hamilton and that was prominently displayed with the rest of the collection. The whole display was opened to the public with a special reception in May of 1963.

This extraordinary collection has remained intact and has been added to over the years, eventually being moved to the second floor mezzanine along with the donated art work. A few months after the collection was received, Frank Johnson who was a member of the library's art committee and a personal friend of Angel, announced that his original drawing of "The Purchase of Newtown from the Indians," was on permanent loan from the Danbury Hospital. It was hung on the wall in the foyer of the old building where the original circulation desk once stood.

The reception of the Angel collection gave added momentum to the library's developing art collection. The library had been a repository for antiques and historical relics since its inception. Along with those artifacts, the library, from time to time, was also given works by local artists and shortly after it began operation, the trustees formed an art committee to curate those works and arrange for periodic exhibitions of local artists' work. The chairman of this committee at the time of the acquisition of the Angel collection was Henry Schnakenberg, who was a nationally known artist in his own right.

Schnakenberg had been born on Staten Island in 1892 and had studied under Kenneth Hayes Miller at the Student Art League in New York City. He later taught at the League and from 1932 served as its president. He also held an honorary Doctor of Fine Arts degree from the University of Vermont. Over the course of his career he had more than a dozen one-man shows at the Whitney Studio Club beginning in 1921 and eighteen such shows at the Kraushaar Galleries in New York. His works appear in many private collections both here and abroad and they hang in the Metropolitan Museum of Art, the Whitney Museum, the Wadsworth Atheneum in Hartford, the Pennsylvania Museum of Fine Arts, the Nebraska Museum of Fine Arts, the Chicago Art Institute, and the Yale University collections. In 1926, the Whitney Club asked him to make a search for American primitive folk art. At the time this was a genre that was almost completely ignored by the art world, but the collection he put together became the nucleus of the Whitney's collection, a collection which established the vogue for American folk art.

Locally Schnakenberg was a charter member of the Newtown Historical Society and it was he who arranged for a fund-raising tour of eighteen studios of local artists including his own. He was also active in and donated to the Newtown Forest Association. But he was probably most closely associated with the library where he served as a trustee from 1956 until his death in 1970. From his position as chairman of the art committee he arranged for several spectacular art shows featuring other nationally-known artists who lived in Newtown.

One of these was Stockton Mulford. Mulford had been born in 1886 in Pennsylvania but at a very young age his family had moved to Portland, Oregon. He had attended the Portland Academy, but returned to the East to attend the Student's Art League in New York, where, coincidently, he came to know Schnakenberg. He became a well-known freelance magazine illustrator, his work appearing frequently on the cover and in the pages of *Saturday Evening Post*, *Liberty*, *Red Book*, and *Cosmopolitan*. He was probably best known for his book illustrations for the *Tarzan* and *Pollyana* series. Through

Schnakenberg's influence, Mulford held a show of his illustrations. (Many years earlier his wife, who was a locally prominent artist, held a one-women show of local landscapes.) In 1961, a year after his death, Mrs. Mulford presented the library with a painting entitled *The Yule Log*, which features a slave family with the father carrying a Yule log toward the fire. The caption indicated that it was a standard practice among slave masters to allow his slaves to enjoy time off over Christmas until the Yule log was consumed. The practice with this slave family was to put the log out every night to make it last longer and prolong the holiday. This work now hangs in the library director's office.

Rea Irvin was another nationally known artist whose works formed one of the art chairman's first exhibits in 1956. Irvin was born in San Francisco in 1896 and by age fifteen he was drawing cartoons for the *San Francisco Examiner*. He moved on to the *San Francisco Post* and then to the *Honolulu Advertiser* where his salary reached the munificent sum of $25 a week. By 1924 he was in New York and quickly established a local reputation for his cartoon art which was sufficient to earn him the position of art director for *Life* magazine when it was still a humor magazine.

In early 1925, Harold Ross was setting up *The New Yorker* and convinced Irvin to become his art director. He accepted and one of his first tasks was to design the cover of the premier issue, which was going to be launched in February. Irvin developed a stylized drawing of a haughty Victorian dandy with a high stock collar, a ridiculously large quill pen in his right hand, a sheaf of papers in his left, and a monocle screwed into his left eye. This character became known as Eustace Tilley and it served as a trademark of the magazine. Every anniversary of the founding issue, this cover would be repeated.

This cover was his start with the publication that he would be associated with for the rest of his life and bring him into contact with the immortals of the east coast literary scene including E. B. White and James Thurber, the latter of which had his own Newtown connection. In 1965, Schnakenberg convinced Irvin to mount an exhibition consisting primarily of his cover art for *The*

New Yorker. Three years later, one of those cover paintings was donated to the library and it remains one of the most valuable pieces in the library's collection.

One of the strangest art exhibits was mounted after Schnakenberg's death, and it consisted of the doodles of James Thurber. For several years in the 1930s Thurber owned one of the old Curtis houses on Riverside Road. Most of his time was still spent in New York but the Newtown house became a weekend retreat. He also did some of his writing here and for that purpose he turned one of the upstairs rooms into a study. Thurber was an incurable doodler and wherever a free surface presented itself, it would soon be covered with Thurber drawings. He filled the walls of the bathroom at *The New Yorker* with such drawings, which so aggravated Harold Ross that he had them painted over, only to find that Thurber considered the newly painted walls new canvas upon which he could work. The walls of Thurber's study were no exception, but when he became estranged from his wife and she inherited the house she promptly had the drawings wallpapered over.

It was only in the 1970s when the new owners of the house were remodeling the old study that they stripped off the wallpaper to find a treasure of Thurberian art. The discovery immediately created a sensation. The decision was finally made to preserve the drawings by taking them, plaster and all, off of the wall and giving them to Thurber's alma mater Ohio State University. Before they left town, however, the library arranged for them to be displayed in the reference room between Thanksgiving and Christmas of 1976. The town was delighted with cartoons of the Sandy Hook Band in which Thurber once played, various of his dogs doing very undogful things, and where there was a crack in the plaster, a little man with a banner reading "Excelsior" could be seen strenuously climbing toward what would have been the ceiling. It is unfortunate that these art gems could not have stayed in town but this only slightly diminishes the art treasures that the library has been able to preserve from the town's locally and nationally known artists.

The Sarah Mitchell - Betty Downs Years

Sarah Mitchell served as head librarian from 1955 to 1971 after years of being acting head librarian. In 1961, Elizabeth "Betty" Downs was hired and Mitchell, seeing her obvious ability and enthusiasm for the library, became her mentor. By 1964, Betty was made assistant librarian as she continued to serve as an apprentice. Thus by 1971, when Sarah Mitchell retired, Downs was ready to take over and steer the library through the next decade.

Sarah Mitchell

For most of the Mitchell - Downs years the library remained relatively unchanged; so much so that in a 1973 *Bee* article on the library's history, the reporter pointedly remarked that the library had changed little since it had opened. This did not mean that there was no change at all; there were small changes, such as the acquisition of an Auto Page Drop Box. This was purchased from the Thomaston Library in April 1972 and installed on the driveway at the rear of the building where patrons could leave material after hours. A major change occurred at the beginning of 1970 when a photocopier was installed in the main entry. This was primarily to serve patrons using the genealogy collection whose valuable volumes were in danger of being mutilated by enthusiastic family hunters whose family was treated in long passages that were time consuming to copy out by hand.

One of the greatest additions to the library volunteer staff during this time was Hilda Ferris. Because of the Julia Brush Collection, the library had become known as a regional center for genealogical research. As a result, it had been receiving genealogical queries from all over the country. Unfortunately the staff had neither the time nor the expertise to do the sometime extensive searching that these queries demanded. Since Ferris had always been a knowledgeable and enthusiastic genealogist she volunteered to respond to these out-of-town letters beginning in July of 1969. Since she was frequently in the genealogy room tending to those responses, she also helped those who just stopped in hoping to find ancestors and family members.

In 1976 for the nation's bicentennial, Ferris began a project that would have a profound impact on the study of Newtown's local history and genealogy. She began indexing the back issues of *The Newtown Bee*. The morgue for *The Bee* had been in the basement vault of the library since the 1930s. This archive of Newtown news was continuous since they first began binding each year of the newspaper in 1892. (The newspaper had been in continuous publication since 1877, but the pre-1892 issues had not been saved by the paper's editor Reuben H. Smith. It was preserved under his brother and successor, Allison Smith.)

Mrs. Ferris began with the January 1, 1892 issue and began copying into a three-ring binder the headlines or brief statement of content of every article pertaining to Newtown, followed by a general subject area. Driven by her genealogical proclivities, she also recorded all of the vital records (births, marriages, and deaths) in a special section of her notebook. Periodically, a member of the staff would take these notebook entries and type them onto three-by-five index cards and then slip them into a card file. She continued to work on this project until 1986, shortly before her death. The final product was a ninety-four-year chronological listing of all of the news that was pertinent to Newtown which has made possible the historical research of the town historian as well as that of *The Newtown Bee* staff, and even the production of this history. She produced all of this for the munificent sum of one dollar an hour.

These changes left the structure and procedures of the library essentially the same as they had been for the previous fifty years. However, the quarter century of the Mitchell - Downs period were years of substantial growth. The collection increased seventy percent to over 38,000 volumes, but the circulation just about tripled to almost 100,000 items. More incredibly, the number of cardholders quadrupled to just under 10,000, reflecting the rapid population increases that the town experience in the 1960s and 1970s as it became a true suburb of Danbury and Bridgeport. This type of growth created pressures especially on the facilities. The collection could not grow to meet the continually rising demand in the limited space of a building that was designed to comfortably hold only 25,000 volumes.

**Betty Downs shown here accepting a token
of appreciation at her retirement in 1981**

Betty Downs, along with the board of trustees, had begun to deal with these growing pains as plans were being formulated to expand the library, but they were just in the beginning stages in 1981 when she retired. Regrettably, her successor, Dennis Clark, was not up to the challenges of the new era. He was a professionally trained librarian, came with good recommendations and he interviewed well, but once on the job his management skills proved weak and he had trouble dealing with the pressures created by the mounting demands for change. Within a year he was led to submit his resignation, and Janet Woycik, the recently hired children's librarian, was advanced to the position of head librarian.

Janet Woycik

Mrs. Woycik was a native of Brewster, New York. She had completed a bachelor's degree in education at Western Connecticut State College, and a master's degree in library science at Arizona State University. Returning to Newtown in 1976, she remained active in the local schools both as a substitute teacher and active member of the local PTA. She also served as the supervisor of the Educational Communication Center at RESCUE in Litchfield, through which she maintained contact with both the local schools and libraries. Through this connection she learned of the position of children's librarian that had opened up in 1981. She was hired on her birthday, December 1, and then elevated to acting head librarian in July of the next year and to head librarian three months later. Her acceptance of the head library post was done understanding the library's problems and she rose to the challenges, successfully piloted the institution through its major expansion, through the sometime difficult process of modernization. Under her guidance came the quantum leap in technology that the library would experience over the last twenty years of the twentieth century. She has become the longest serving head librarian in the library's history, a period which can truly be considered, "The Woycik Years."

~ *Chapter Six* ~

Expansion and Modernization

The idea of expanding the library was not new. It had been percolating more and more fiercely as the collection and circulation numbers grew, but the building which had been on the cutting edge of libraries in the 1930s, had features that made it difficult to expand, especially in light of the modern fire codes. The upstairs galleries, which appeared to be ideal space into which to expand the collection, were not suitable to a fire code that demanded at least two means of egress from any public space. By the 1980s the expedient of an external fire escape was not acceptable, which is just as well since this solution would have created ugly excrescences hanging off the north and south sides of the building. In addition it was found that the steel-reinforced concrete floors were not meant to support full stacks of books. Engineers cautioned that books should only be shelved along the walls where there was greater support. The answer seemed to be to add a wing, but this initially created such a firestorm of negative public comment that the library would have to take half-way measures for twenty years before the building was properly expanded and modernized.

The First Expansion Attempts

The first discussions of adding fire escapes to allow public access began as early as 1974. In response to those discussions, the library's architect determined that the cost of $104,000 would yield only enough space to allow for a brief period of expansion after which point the library would again be facing the same problem that the fire escapes were to solve. In other words, they simply were not cost effective. Similarly, the construction of enclosed external stairways, although it would result in a more aesthetic solution, was even more expensive than the fire escapes and would result in the same cost inefficiency.

The discussion continued for the next two years before the trustees realized that the only long term answer would be an addition. By the second half of 1976, Bruce Falconer, who had been retained by the board to come up with initial designs for expansion, had worked out several options. By the beginning of the next year these had been whittled down to one plan that would just about double the floor space with an addition that would extend to the south of the old building. In June of 1977, the board set up a building committee and engaged the architectural firm of Moore and Salisbury of Avon to develop drawings of the new addition and assist in presenting these plans to the town. The sum of $8,500 was appropriated from the library's internal funds to pay for this and by August 14, architect Alex Frost had submitted plans that were quickly approved. Meanwhile, the library had received a $56,000 construction grant from the State Development Office which would be applied against the $700,000 estimated total cost of the project. From such an auspicious start, the road to addition quickly became very rocky.

With all of the publicity and public presentation made by the building committee, a large faction of Newtown's citizens could not see the logic in building an addition that would meet the needs of the town into the next millennium. In the public forum of *The Newtown Bee's* Letter Hive, letters continued to demand that the library board first expend whatever money necessary to expand into the second story. The delays caused by the public debate in the legislative council and selectmen's meetings began to jeopardize the construction grant as the deadline for groundbreaking grew closer. The delays also led the architects to abandon the entire Newtown project. Fortunately Norman Baier from the firm of Gallagher and Schoenardt of New Hartford stepped in and picked up the planning and promotion process.

The complicated political machinations involved in the process of trying to get the proposed addition approved by the town are not worth detailed treatment since they were unsuccessful in the end. The process did, however, get to the bid stage and one contractor who was hungry for this job came in with a remarkable bid of under one million dollars, substantially below the rest. With this good news the selectmen went before the town with a referendum in early 1980, which went down to defeat. When the library addition was finally successful about fifteen years later, the cost would come in at more than four times the 1980 bid.

The unsuccessful expansion efforts still left the board of trustees with the problem of burgeoning demands on library services. Even before the failure of the referendum, plans were underway to buy shelving and expand the stack space into the main floor north reading rooms. The fiction section was moved into that room and the reference collection was set up in the south reading room.

At this point, responding to the public's demand to utilize the upstairs galleries, the building committee began working with local architect Stephen Griss, to develop plans utilizing as much of that upstairs space as the engineers thought to be safe. The fire codes would be a primary force in developing these plans, but by this time concern for handicap access was also a factor. The new plans called for a small addition to the rear of the building that would accommodate an elevator. Two short corridors would then be built into the west walls of the two upstairs galleries giving a second means of egress from each of the rooms. The cost for all of this was a little over $200,000, which by the end of 1984, yielded a larger children's room in the south gallery and a young adult room in the north gallery. In both of these books could be shelved along the walls leaving the center areas for short book shelves and places for children to sit for story hours and other juvenile entertainments.

Success

A decade would pass before the idea of expanding the library would again be raised. Meanwhile, extensive repairs were made to the old slate roof, the chimneys on both sides of the building were rebuilt, and the downstairs meeting room was refurbished with funds from the estate of Bertram Strook. But during this decade the library experienced the revival of the same growing pains that had compelled the earlier failed attempts to expand. By 1993, the collection had more than doubled to 68,000 volumes and circulation had increased over thirty percent. The memory of the last expansion attempt, however, was so traumatic that on May 9, 1993, there was actually an extended debate over leaving the present site and building a new library elsewhere. The traditionalists prevailed and the process of planning a new addition began.

The process got underway with a feasibility study performed by the firm of King and Tuttle. In November, the consensus was to expand to the rear with an addition that would about double the building's floor space. Behind this consensus was the driving idea that the library expansion had to be targeted to meet library needs twenty-five years into the future, and the rearward addition clearly addressed that. By January of 1994 it was agreed that the board would submit a request that the town add $3.8 million dollars to its five-year capital plan.

The experience with poor public relations ten years earlier had been a powerful lesson for the board and with the new expansion underway plans were made to avoid earlier mistakes. In mid-1994 an appropriation of $51,000 was voted to pay J. Donovan Associates, "for the purpose of bringing the concept of the addition to the entire community and to express the need of the community for the proposed addition." A month later a video tape promoting the addition was made and offered to anyone who would play it at a public venue. Two members of the board taped an interview for presentation on the cable's public access Channel 21 for repeated airings over a four-month period. Invitations to speak about the library expansion before twenty-one local civic organizations were solicited and various members of the board were delegated to spread the expansion gospel. While this was in process the formal process of getting approval from the various town boards was begun. By May of 1995 the Public Building Committee had formally approved the plans. During that same month lawsuits were launched against the library to stop the expansion, most notably by the library's southern neighbor, Ed Baumer.

By the end of 1995 approvals from the various town agencies had been received. Bids for the project had been received and opened, a contractor selected, and a town meeting for the approval of the library expansion was scheduled. The public relations efforts along with the changes in the building that the library board had implemented after the earlier expansion failure, had blunted the saber of the expansion opponents and the proposition passed both the town meeting and the inevitable referendum. The legal efforts to halt construction, however, continued until February 13, 1996, when the suits were denied. At 5:30 P.M. on March 18, the board participated in a grand groundbreaking ceremony followed by a reception.

There is a general rule of construction that the process will never proceed without problems and delays. The library project was no exception. The construction schedule had been worked out so that the library would continue to supply services as long as possible while the preparation work and construction of the rear addition was well underway. The library would then close while the two structures were joined and the finish work was being done. The discovery of asbestos in the old building changed all of that.

On October 8, the board met in emergency session; the old plaster walls, it was discovered, contained a one percent mixture of asbestos which had been done to confer fireproofing. This was not a problem when the walls were undisturbed, but when construction broke through parts of the old basement walls, the dust released contained the carcinogen and the staff and public could no longer be in the building. The board needed $42,000 for asbestos abatement which was taken from contingency funds and the library was closed completely. The renovation and addition were on hold until the asbestos was abated.

In order to keep the town from losing library services completely, a series of contingency plans were drawn up. Even before the asbestos problem had developed, it was arranged for the staff to move to the recently vacated A&P building in the Queen Street Shopping Center where minimal services were offered. By the end of 1996 this awkward arrangement could no longer be sustained and through the efforts of Rep. Julia Wasserman, arrangements were made with the state to utilize part of Fairfield Hills Hospital. In February 1997, the move was made to the southwest wing of Shelton House and for the next eight months the reading public wandered through the dormitory rooms and sun parlor of the old reception building where mental patients had been registered, diagnosed, and assigned to longer term treatment. Meanwhile, the library staff tried to meet the public's need for reading matter and information with what few available resources they had and with most of the book collection in storage containers back on the library grounds.

The major problems were solved and the addition proceeded somewhat behind schedule. By September 9 Janet Woycik announced that the move into the new facility would begin on September 22 and would take three to five weeks. Murphy's Law of Construction was again at work when the storage containers were opened and it was discovered that they were not watertight. Portions of the collection had been irreparably water damaged. Delay over insurance settlements extended the estimated five weeks to the end of the year, but finally on January 11, 1998, between 1:00 and 5:00 P.M. the public was welcomed into its new library. With punch and cookies in hand, townspeople watched as the first selectmen who had served during expansion process, Robert Cascella and Herb Rosenthal, ceremoniously cut the ribbon and allowed the assembled masses to wander through a state-of-the-art library facility which so many had worked so hard on for so long.

The Library Reorganizes

Until 1981 the Cyrenius H. Booth Library had been entirely self-sustaining. It received no tax money from the town, existing solely on the interest generated from the Hawley Trust Fund, and from other funds that had been set up from bequests or transferred from the old John Beach Library. In recent years, some money had been raised by direct appeal to the public in annual fund-raising efforts, but the town formally supplied nothing except coverage on the town's insurance policies. This independence created the impression among the public that the library was an insular and somewhat haughty institution with an exclusive board of trustees that was not responsive to public opinion.

During the height of the first expansion attempt, the library was faced with the necessity of applying to the town for a budget line item to help cover operational expenses. The trust funds were not yielding revenue as they once had and the library needed more money to cover salaries as well as for modernization and to fund the preliminaries for expansion. The barometer of public opinion, the Letter Hive of *The Newtown Bee*, however, let the library board know that they were not favorably disposed to giving funds to the library, unless it would restructure itself to be more responsive to the public and its elective bodies. As a result, the library instituted the most sweeping reorganization since it had opened in 1931.

According to the original charter, the board of trustees consisted of twenty-four members who were elected into trustee positions by a vote of the rest of the trustees. Once elected, they served an unlimited term. This is why Anna May Betts and Alice Carroll, who had been on the original board of trustees, continued to serve on the board until 1976 and 1987 respectively.

Changes in the by-laws, which went into effect in July of 1982, began by paring the board down to eighteen members who would serve a term of three years. These three-year terms would be served in rotation so that every year six board members would be voted on to serve another term as trustee. Further, the number of consecutive terms any trustee could serve was limited to three. After nine years the member had to absent himself for two years before being readmitted to the board.

The most drastic change embodied in the new by-laws, however, provided for political representation. The board had always been non-partisan and non-political. Starting in 1982, six seats on the board would be set aside to be appointed by the first selectman with the approval of the legislative council. In addition, three of these political appointees would be Republican and three would be Democrat. When any one of these trustees left the board he or she had to be replaced with another appointment from the same party. In this way the governing body of the library made itself slimmer and more efficient, while becoming more politically responsive to the public. Without these changes, the ultimate expansion and modernization of the library would have never occurred.

Library Custodian Jim Kearns

While the library was expanding and modernizing it is important to note that the library had only five custodians in its seventy-five year history. Jim Kearns was in charge of maintaining the building for thirty-one of those years, from 1967 to 1998, making him the longest-serving custodian as well as the most dedicated.

The Friends of the Library and Its Fabled Book Sale

The history of the Labor Day Book Sale and the Friends of the Cyrenius H. Booth Library are inextricably intertwined. A library Friends' organization is normally a support group for the library, supplying volunteers and financial aid. Most of these organizations are formed by the library staff or board of trustees, and after being established and incorporated, begin fund-raising activities which frequently includes the sale of books, both donated "pre-owned" books and library discards, and the publication of fund-raising new books such as cook books. In Newtown's case, all of this happened in reverse. Fund-raising in the form of book sales came first and the Friends grew out of that.

Although annual book sales began in the early 1970s the idea of selling used books from the library went back to 1952. In the annual meeting for that year, Mary Lucas reported that she had raised $106.75. "During the summer months in order to make space on the shelves, we tried the experiment of selling books at 5 and 10 cents; also copies of 'Newtown's Bicentennial'." (The copies of *Newtown's Bicentennial* were the remainders left over from 1905!) This process of selling off library discards continued for the next two decades yielding not much more than that first year. Most of the books were sold from two bookcases that had been set up in the front foyer, just to the left as one came through the front door. Here was an ever-changing spectrum of subjects, in various states of disrepair, but usually available for less than one dollar.

In 1956 Sarah Mitchell reported that there had been a series of books given as gifts to the library, and with these gifts began a new policy regarding the flow of books into the library's holdings. Among these gifts were many that could not be used in the collection or were duplicates of books already there, so they were offered for sale during the summer months. This policy has continued and has become the basis for the present acceptance of books by the library and a source of supply to the modern book sales.

On September 7, 1974, the first Labor Day book sale was held and it soon became a regularly scheduled event. This first sale was initiated by Joanne Zang who became the guiding force behind book sales for the next thirty years and beyond. That first year she decided that the books which had accumulated in the front foyer could be better disposed of by setting up a card table in front of the library during the Labor Day Parade when the flow of people in front of the building was greatest. Her instincts were accurate and she realized $35 from her first card-table sale.

In the same month that Joanne reported her success, the first mention of the Friends of the C.H. Booth Library appears in the trustees' minutes. Anne Gushee, who would become president of the board two years later, and Betty Downs were asked by the trustees to look into forming such a support group. By November they had about thirty women who were interested and on November 17 at 3:00 P.M. they had their first organizational meeting. Within a year and a half they set up and supplied volunteers for a number of ancillary library programs such as a preschool story hours for children and a bookmobile to bring books to seniors. In addition they introduced a film series and coffee discussion hour which coincided with the story hours for the convenience of the mothers. Christmas and Halloween parties were also organized for the children. To make these programs possible, money was needed and this was supplied from member dues and from various fund-raisers, most notable of which was the Labor Day book sale, which Joanne Zang continued to direct as a member of the Friends.

All organizations go through cycles of greater and lesser energy that mark their relative successes and failures. The Friends operated successfully for about eight years. Then with the reduction and renovation of the board in 1981 and the problems with the head librarian, Dennis Clark, the Friends were not getting the support they needed to sustain their creative energies. In addition many of those who had been instrumental in running the organization were running out of energy and were not being replaced with "new blood." In a *Bee* article marking the fiftieth anniversary of the library there was an article dedicated to the Friends, noting that although they were presently disbanded, this was seen as temporary and that many of the popular programs, such as the book sale would continue.

The hiatus lasted nine years. On November 12, 1991, Joanne Zang who had seen to the continuation of the Labor Day book sale over this quiescent period, along with Diane Bowler appeared before the board as representatives of the newly reconstituted Friends of the C.H. Booth Library. By July of the next year they had reestablished the Friends' legal status, elected co-presidents

John Warner and Joanne Zang, incorporated and applied for a Federal Tax ID number. The Friends were back in business with renewed energy that has lasted to the present.

At the November 12 board meeting, a very important policy regarding the relationship between the Friends and the library board was established, one that would frequently be reiterated. The Friends was an autonomous organization whose funds were not to become part of the library budget. By asserting this they resisted the attempts by the town's budget creators and those who opposed the library budget for whatever reason, to lump the Friends treasury into the library assets and then reduce the line item for the library in the town budget. The assertion of this principle became even more important as the fund-raisers they sponsored grew successful and the coffers of the organization swelled.

Later in the same year that the Friends reestablished their legal status, it published the first of the *Newtown Trails Books*. These books developed from a project initiated by Mary Mitchell and Albert Goodrich, two close friends who enjoyed hiking, exploring nature, and local history. Al was a retired engineer whose love was maps. He drew the trail maps after both of them repeatedly walked the trails. Mary, an accomplished and published author, then added text which included information about the trails and another feature not found in most other trail-books, something about the history of the area through which the trails ran.

The trails book ultimately went through five editions which included updates on existing trails and new trails that had come into existence since the previous edition. The second edition included a unique feature: Newtown Rail Trails. Recognizing that the defunct railroad rights-of-way were ideal hiking trails, they proceeded to map those that were available to the public. Mary's historical notes on each of the five rail lines that once passed through Newtown made the second and subsequent editions virtual histories of railroading in Newtown. Her discovery of Hawleyville as a rail hub through which all five lines and 153 trains a day passed at the turn of the twentieth century not only startled her readers and Newtown's hikers, but her discoveries of the people such as A.G. Baker the furniture magnate, and William Upham, the inventor of the tea bag, added a historical sense to their tours that took hikers away from the strict natural history treatments of other trail guides and introduced the human element as a positive part of the environment.

The trail books were not completely without problems. In 1999, a neighbor who lived next to the Purdy Station pegmatite mine, became irate that the Mitchell-Goodrich maps showed a public right of way to the mine that ran adjacent to their property. The attacks on the authors, the library, and the Friends as the publishers of the books finally resulted in a lawsuit in which anyone who had anything to do with its publication were either named or issued a subpoena to appear in court. This assault on two people who had done so much for the town produced an outpouring of sympathy and a group of local lawyers took on the case of all of those who were named in the suit on a pro bono basis. The case was settled before going to trial, but the agreement reached was sealed, so the outcome is still unknown. The books continue to sell well but without the offending map which the authors had removed from the books after the first complaint.

The big and steady fund-raiser, however, continued to be the Labor Day book sale. By the 1990s the sale had grown dramatically. In 1990, alone, it raised over $22,000 and it had more then doubled by 1996. Up until that year, the sale had been held in the library building, spreading to a series of tents on the back lawn as the number of donated books outgrew the building's interior space. In 1996, however, the building was beginning its renovation and was not available nor was the back lawn because of construction equipment. That year it was temporarily moved to the old defunct A&P in the Queen Street Shopping Center, spreading from the interior of the old store out into the parking lot. The next year the venue became the biggest enclosed space in Newtown: Bridgeport Hall at the closed Fairfield Hills Hospital.

That year (1996) was a banner year for the sale of the trails book, having realized over $10,000. It was also notable for the

Sarah Booth Cookbook. This developed out of the discovery of Mary Hawley's mother's cookbook in the Hawley papers. This was edited, the recipes tested, and the result published as a fund-raiser. In 1997 it went into a second printing and was featured in the *New York Times.* It also won a $100 prize in a national contest sponsored by the Tabasco Company.

In 1998 a local book store, The Book Review, closed. A total of 8,000 new books were donated by it to the Friends and the book sale realized a new record of $58,000. In addition, the previous year the Friends again began selling books in nearly new or new condition in a section of bookcases to the left of the main circulation desk that became known as "The Book Nook." This resulted in a steady stream of income over the course of the year which in 1998 amounted to $6,000.

Finally by 2003 the proceeds of the book sale reached a record of $113,289 with over 150,000 books offered for sale, making the Newtown book sale the largest on the east coast. Unfortunately in 2005, Bridgeport Hall was being renovated for use by the town and was unavailable to the Friends. This left the dilemma of finding a space that could handle the gargantuan number of books. Not having the sale at all was seriously considered, but this would leave an impossible mountain of books that had to be disposed of somehow. The solution was to utilize Newtown Hall in the entry plaza of the closed Fairfield Hills Hospital for the rare collections, and erect a large tent in the parking lot for the bulk of the books. This was not an ideal solution since the tent could not be completely sealed from the rain showers that plagued that holiday weekend. The total realized from the sale was a respectable $95,000, but it was down from the previous two years.

The 2006 solution was to use the auditorium and gymnasium of the recently constructed Reed Intermediate School. This provided an air-conditioned and adequate environment but it forced the sale date to be moved. Since Labor Day was after the beginning of the school year, the sale had to be moved to the Fourth of July weekend. This provided a very limited amount of time for set-up but with a massive volunteer effort, the sale was ready in time. In 2007, the sale was again scheduled in the Reed Intermediate School for the weekend before the Fourth of July. Unfortunately, in May the town suffered from a category F1 tornado which resulted in property destruction, massive power outages, and the closing of the schools for two days. This reduced the time of set-up for the book sale by two days. The book sale volunteers were equal to the task and with Herculean efforts the book sale was ready to open on its appointed day, and the gross revenue from the sale exceeded that of the previous year. The book sale, as the Friends who sustain it, have survived the adversities of size and time and have become an essential part of the library.

The Antiques Reference Library

R. Scudder Smith, after coming to work at *The Newtown Bee*, indulged his love of antiques and primitive art by creating a weekly supplement to the newspaper dedicated to antiques of all kinds. By 1976, this had become an independent newspaper called *Antiques and the Arts Weekly*, and its circulation became national. The prominence of this paper attracted complementary copies of almost every new book on antiques and American art in hopes that they would lead to a favorable review. The direct consequence of this phenomenon was a large collection of books which cluttered the limited space of *The Bee* office.

By 1990 the problem had become so acute that it led to the formation of the Antiques Reference Library. This coincided with *The Bee's* purchase of the Red Brick Building on Main Street in which the collection was to be housed. This two-story building had been constructed in 1855 to house the offices of the town clerk and probate office and provide safe storage for some of the town's most important records. The upper story, which was only accessible by an outside staircase on the south side of the building, served various purposes over the course of the years including a home for the Newtown Library before the construction of the John Beach Memorial building. In recent times an interior staircase had been built and the exterior staircase removed. With some renovation, it became suitable for a library on the ground floor with a meeting room and lounge upstairs. It was also renamed the Scudder Building.

The Antiques Reference Library continued to increase in size over the course of the next decade until it had become a formidable collection of reference books on all areas of antiques, art, and the process of collecting. It included both scholarly works and popular guides which gave readers the identifying characteristics of antiques and collectibles along with approximate prices. The collection also contained a small collection of works relating to Newtown's history which had collected at *The Bee* office over the years.

After the books were transferred to the building, cataloged, and entered into the computer, the antiques library was open one day a week with a librarian in attendance, and at other times by appointment, after securing the key at *The Bee* offices. Unfortunately, the limited access and the limited knowledge of its existence meant that it was not used as extensively as the Antiques Reference Library's board of trustees had hoped. By 2001, the board felt that the collection would be more accessible if housed across the street in the Cyrenius H. Booth Library.

Accordingly, on October 9, a letter was sent to the library board offering to donate the collection if space could be found to keep the collection intact, together, and properly designated with an appropriate book plate. The offer was accepted and the upstairs north gallery was designated as its home. Over the next year the Reference Librarians Beryl Harrison and Andrea Zimmermann, and staff member Elizabeth Conti re-cataloged the books and entered them into the library's computer system. This was the last major collection received by the library and its installation gave patrons another magnificent resource for those seriously interest in antiques or just interested in identifying a treasure recently acquired at a tag sale. This resource, along with the Angel Art Collection, and the Brush Genealogical and Local History Collection, has turned the C.H. Booth Library into a unique research facility and one that the citizens of Newtown can be justifiably proud.

The Technological Revolution

Beginning with Janet Woycik's term as head librarian, the library underwent a technological revolution. The technology, which completely changed the way the library was run, at first ranged from the simple introduction of photocopiers as early as 1970 to the introduction of circulating videotapes in 1986, and then centered on the conversion of the library's information systems to the computer, and that began with the introduction of Bibliomation.

Bibliomation was an early computer network centered in Bridgeport, which had been set up by a group of computer and library professionals in southwestern Connecticut. It consisted of seventeen libraries whose collective card catalogues were available on each member's computers. A desired book could be located in the collections of any of the participants. Requests could then be made and the person making the request could visit the library that had the book and check it out, or could wait for it to be shipped to the library from which the request was made, a process that was included in the service and which could be done in three days or less.

Interest in Bibliomation began with an assessment of the Newtown collection conducted by Anne Lee, a library consultant to the state. In 1984 the library had a collection of about 35,000 volumes and was rapidly reaching its capacity of 40,000. A community the size of Newtown, however, should have a collection of 70,000 to adequately serve it. A quick study of the possibility of making the collection adequate to the recommendations concluded that about $700,000 would be necessary for books and whatever space was necessary to house them, but with the rapid growth of the town's population, even that effort would rapidly become inadequate. Bibliomation, however, would give the library patron instant access to over 750,000 books turning the library into a "first class library that can satisfy any patron."

The discussion among board members began at their January 10, 1984 meeting and centered on the cost. The desirability of the service was unanimously agreed upon, but there would be a $35,000 one-time entrance fee and then an annual fee or service charge of $10,000 to $14,000. There would also be a one-time cost for the two necessary computer terminals. In addition it would take at least a year to prepare the library for the system because all of the library's holdings had to be entered into the Bibliomation data bank. This would involve one temporary paid staff addition, although most of the work, it was felt, could be accomplished by volunteers. After the usual extensive discussion, the board voted unanimously to join the system.

The project of getting the library onto the network was ultimately done completely by volunteers. Jackie Maskell, herself a volunteer, gathered thirty volunteers by November 1984 and spent one to two hours with each volunteer to train them in data entry. The volunteers then spent several hours a week working on the computers. Meanwhile, the library staff was trained over the summer, telephone lines were run into the building and the computer terminals were set up. The final part of the project was to reregister all of the library patrons and issue them a new Bibliomation card so they could access the system. All of this took longer than was expected but by September 1986 the library was finally on-line and functioning at a far more advanced level than ever before.

A by-product of the Bibliomation process was the computerization of the process of checking library materials in and out. While the library's books were being entered onto the Bibliomation database, a unique bar code was added to each volume. The patron's new cards also carried a bar code that identified him so that with the card scanned into the computer, followed by the bar code of the desired books, the patron was checked out in a matter of seconds rather than minutes which were required by the old paper-and-book-card system. In addition, the computer automatically kept a record of all of the books checked out, could flag when books were overdue, and allow patrons to locate a book with a few key strokes and the press of the "enter" key rather than a lengthy session thumbing through index cards in the card catalog. The computer screen also notified the searcher immediately if the book being searched for was in the library or checked out, and, although it was not possible to find out who the person was who had borrowed the book, the date it was due back was available.

While the Bibliomation process was going forward, computers were invading other aspects of the library operation. On July 9, 1985, the board voted to spend the $2,000 gift that had been given by the Borough of Newtown on a computer for the use of the public. It was decided that they would purchase an Apple IIe computer and that it would be used primarily in the children's room. A year later, the newly elected treasurer, Ted Kreinik, requested and received computer software to be used in bookkeeping and budget matters.

By 1991 computers were in general use throughout the library both for library operations and for patron use. At the March 1991 board meeting, Reference Librarian Beryl Harrison demonstrated the use of InfoTrac, a magazine database, and ReQuest, the statewide library catalog, which were now connected to the Internet. This marked a major advance in the research capabilities of the library since now vast amounts of data in almost any field could be retrieved online, and done so very quickly. But this advance increased the demand for greater computer capacity. By late 1997, the reference librarians presented the finance committee with a new computer network plan for the new library addition. This included building a computer network from scratch, wiring the building and purchasing computers and printers for the staff and public. The plan was estimated to cost $104,050, but this would be offset by a $53,000 donation from the Friends of the Library. The affluence created by the ever-increasing success of the book sale was beginning to pay substantial dividends for the library.

The Internet had first come to the library through its new computer network in 1998. With its increasing popularity, the dark side of the Internet began to appear. It could be used for research, but the accuracy of the data harvested had to be carefully evaluated, something of which many early users were not fully aware. There were also sites that were completely inappropriate in the library setting and some especially so for minors. The Internet frequently took the reference personnel away from their other duties to fix problems and glitches to which the Internet was frequently err. Staff members often needed to instruct neophyte Internet users on the basics of how to use it. In response, Librarian Woycik drafted an Internet policy in November 1999, which addressed each of these problems and although the problems persisted, the growing sophistication of Internet users obviated many of them.

On December 6, 2005, the latest development in computer network technology was installed: wireless access. This advance, often called WiFi, allowed the user to sign onto the library's wireless network running on a dedicated high-speed cable modem from his own machine after some simple reconfiguring. This meant that one could access the Internet from anywhere in the building, and even from a short distance outside. It is not unusual to see a car drive up close to the back entrance at 11:00 or 12:00 at night and sit there in the suffused glow of a computer laptop while email is being checked.

Patron computers in library reference department, 2007

Over the past decade, further Internet subscription services and Internet features have been be added so that library users now have free access to a world of information unimagined when Bibiomation was first being discussed. This has led some of the town's futurists to scoff at the thought of books, considering them obsolete in light of the Internet which answers all questions and satisfies any need for entertainment. For most who are devoted to the library, however, the thought of curling up in bed with a warm computer is simply not satisfying. For them, the printed word will always be there where it can be accessed instantaneously and cannot be taken away by a power surge, or sudden crash, or other computer catastrophe.

The present library's mix of print material along with an ever-growing collection of video and audio media, and computers that can be used to access audiobooks, mark it as a modern twenty-first century institution, with capabilities that the members of the Newtown Library Association could not even have imagined.

C.H. Booth Library main hall, 2007

What the Newtown Library Association started so hesitantly in 1876 has developed into an immensely satisfying education and entertainment institution, a center for community activity, and arguably the most important building in town.

Library's reading room (right of entrance), 2007

Library's genealogy room (left of entrance), 2007

Young adult collection, 2007

Children's story hour room, 2007

Side entrance featuring sculpture donated by the Friends of the C.H. Booth Library, 2007

APPENDIX

Appendix A

Librarians of the Cyrenius H. Booth Library

1. William N. Strong - 1932 -1933
2. Vera R. Tracy – 1933 -1939
3. Alice P. Davidson (nee Hancock) -1939 -1946
4. Gladys B. Dexter - 1946 - 1948
5. Sarah Mitchell (acting head librarian) 1948 -1951
6. Mary Lucas - 1951 - 1955
7. Sarah Mitchell - 1955 - 1971
8. Betty Downs - 1971 - 1981
9. Dennis Clark - 1981 - 1982
10. Janet Woycik - 1982 -

Appendix B

Officers of the Cyrenius H. Booth Library

Initial Officers: Voted 1931
Arthur T. Nettleton - President
Charles G. Morris - Vice president
Alice Carroll - Secretary
Rodney P. Shepard- Treasurer

President
Arthur T. Nettleton – 1931 -1948
Raymond B. Fosdick - 1948 - 1950
Mortimer Smith - 1950 - 1958
Robert F. Raynolds - 1958 - 1964
Robert J. Clark - 1965 - 1973
Douglas E. Kellogg - 1973 - 1976
Anne Gushee - 1976 - 1978
Herman Jervis - 1978 - 1982

Barbara Phillips - 1982 - 1988
John Warner - 1988 - 1992
Gordon Williams - 1992 – 1998
Jim Larin – 1998 – 2000
Kevin Tepas – July 2000 – Sept. 2000
Joseph Humeston – Sept. 2000 – 2003
Philip Kotch – 2003 - 2004
William Lavery - 2004 -

Vice President
Charles G. Morris - 1931 - 1949
Mortimer Smith - 1949 - 1950
Raymond B. Fosdick - 1950 - 1964
James Brunot - 1964 - 1965
Margaret Warner - 1965 - 1967
Caroline T. White - 1967 - 1969
Mary Holian - 1969 - 1975
Frank L. Johnson -1975 - 1978
Mary Ellen MacDonald - 1978 - 1982
Merlin Fisk - 1982 - 1988
Joanne Zang - 1988 - 1989
Ted Kreinik – 1989 - 1991
Robert Hall – abt. Jan 8, 1991 - Sept 1991
Gordon Williams - 1991 - 1992
Ted Kreinik - 1992 - 1994
Kathy Geckle - 1994 – 1998
Kevin Tepas – 1998 – 2000
Joseph Humeston – 2000 – Sept. 2000
Philip Kotch – 2001 – 2003
Liz Arneth – 2003 – 2004
Kathy Geckle - 2004 – 2006
Martha Robilotti – 2006 -

Secretary
Alice Carroll - 1931 - 1976
Alice Rafferty - 1976 - 1979

Lillian McCarthy - 1979 - 1980
Carole Telfair - 1980 - 1989
Mary Thomas - 1989 - 1991
Pat Denlinger - 1991 – 1997
Karen Schultz – 1997 – 1999
Pat Denlinger – 1999 -

Assistant Secretary
Caroline Stokes - 1975 - 1979

Treasurer
Rodney Shepard - 1931 - 1941
Herbert C. Hubbell - 1941 - 1958
Robert J. Clark - 1958 - 1959
Frank Johnson - 1959 - 1975
Sophia Munger - 1975 - 1977
Charles Travis - 1977 - 1978
James Nevins Hyde - 1978 - 1979
John Friel - 1979 - 1980
Merlin Fisk - 1980 - 1981
Barbara Philips - 1981 - 1982
Kurt Schneider - 1982 - 1985
Ray Marcus - 1985 - 1986
Ted Kreinik - 1986 - 1989
Pat Denlinger - 1989 - 1991
Shelia Allen - 1991 - 1994
Chris Spiro - 1994 – 1998
Joseph Humeston – 1998 – 2000
Richard Sturvedant – 2000 – 2004
Kelly Urso - 2004 - 2007
Peter Marshall - 2007 -

Assistant Treasurer
Sophia Munger - 1977 - 1979

Library Curator
Caroline Stokes - July 1, 1982 to present

Appendix C

Trustees of the Cyrenius H. Booth Library
(Asterik indicates political appointment)

Trustee	Dates of Service	2nd Term
Adams, Kenneth	1980 - 1988	
Alexander, Marilyn	1998 2000	
Allen, Shelia*	1990 - 1995	
Arneth, Liz	2001 -	
Bentley, Lily E.	1931 - 1945	
Betts, Anna M.	1931 - 1976	
Blawie, John	1997 - 2004	
Brew, Thomas F.	1931 - 1955	
Brimmer, Bill	1993 - 1995	
Brody, Seth O.	1957 - 1982	
Broscious, Hamilton*	1999 - 2005	
Brunot, James	1959 - 1976	
Burr, Grace	1949 - 1955	
Carroll, Alice H.	1931 - 1987	
Cheney, Thomas L.	1966 - 1977	
Christensen, Betty	1969 - 1970	
Clark, Robert J.	1931 - 1973	
Clear, Albert	1957 - 1957	
Colt, Charles	1957 - 1974	
Cox, Robert	2002 -	
Cramer, Herbert W.*	1982 - 1989	
Cruson, Daniel	1977 - 1983	2007 -
Curtis, Alice	1955 - 1959	
DaSilva, Eric	2004 -	
Deegan, John	1983 - 1994	
Desmond, Waldo	1939 - 1982	

Denlinger, Patricia	1988 - 1997	1999 -
Domini, Margaret	1964 - 1981	
Driscoll, Ina E.	1931 - 1953	
Farrington, Derby	1939 - 1944	
Faust, Zander	1955 - 1958	
Feld, Rose	1944 - 1975	
Fisk, Merlin	1976 - 1992	1997 - 2003
Foote, William	1967 - 1970	
Fosdick, Raymond B.	1944 - 1965	
Friel, John	1978 - 1980	
Geckle, Kathy	1991 - 2000	2003 -
Goodsell, Frances	1955 - 1968	
Gross, Peggy Jepson	1987 - 1989	
Gushee, Anne	1972 - 1978	
Hall, Raymond	1932 - 1977	
Hall, Robert	1978 - 1992	
Hampton, Sarah R.	1931 - 1957	
Hard, Suzy	1995 - 1999	
Hart, Evelyn M.	1931 - 1949	
Holian, Mary M.	1966 - 1982	
Holian, Thomas M.	1931 - 1939	
Honan, Jeanne*	1986 - 1997	2000 -
Honan, William A.	1931 - 1966	
Hopper, Paula	1994 - 1997	
Howard, Donna	1997 - 2001	
Hubbell, Herbert C.	1931 - 1972	
Humeston, Joseph	1995 - 2005	
Hunter, William	1948 - 1955	
Hyde, James N.	1977 - 1982	
Jackson, Donald	1984 - 1987	
Johnson, Elizabeth	1938 - 1960	
Johnson, Frank L.	1950 - 1982	
Karpacz, Pat*	1982 - 1988	
Kellogg, Douglas	1971 - 1976	
Kotch, Margareta	1995 - 1997	
Kotch, Philip	1999 - 2004	

Kreinik, Ted	1986 - 1996	
Larabee, Dennis	1991 - 1994	
Larin, James	1992 - 2001	
Lasher, Howard	1987 - 1987	
Lavery, Florence*	1988 - 1991	
Lavery, William	1992 - 2002	2004 -
Lux, Catherine	1991 - 1994	
Lyon, Adrienne	1977 - 1977	
MacDonald, Mary Ellen	1973 - 1984	
Madzula, Kathy	1992 - 2001	
Marcus, Raymond	1980 - 1986	
Margulies, Martin	2001 -	
Marshall, Jennie L.	1931 - 1932	
Marshall, Peter	2005 -	
Martin, Juliet	1939 - 1944	
McCarthy, Josephine L.	1931 - 1955	
McCarthy, Lillian	1978 - 1980	
Mead, Sanford	1931 - 1936	
Mills, Esther T.	1931 - 1956	
Morris, Charles G.	1931 - 1958	
Munger, Sophie	1971 - 1981	
Nettleton, Arthur T.	1931 - 1951	
Ojalvo, Dr. Irving*	1982 - 1986	
Osborn, Betty B.	1960 - 1964	
Osborne, Jim	1994 - 1994	
Pankey, Barbara	1977 - 1981	
Parella, Betty	1977 - 1979	
Peck, Abbie L.	1931 - 1941	
Pernell, Mary Elizabeth	1941 - 1943	
Philips, Barbara	1980 - 1990	
Platt, Edmund C.	1931 - 1947	
Platt, Edmund C. Jr.	1952 - 1978	
Post, James	1991 - 1993	
Rafferty, Alice	1970 - 1981	
Ramsey, Alice	1986 - 1987	
Randall, Leslie	1972 - 1977	

Raynolds, Marguerite	1941 - 1982	
Raynolds, Robert	1955 - 1965	
Raynor, Bonnie	1977 - 1979	
Recht, Carol	1999 - 2004	
Reidy, Bernard	1998 - 2000	
Reilly, Jennifer Kurtz	2005 -	
Reynolds, Kate B.	1937 - 1941	
Reynolds, Walter A.	1931 - 1971	
Roberts, Jeane*	1982 - 1991	
Robilotti, Martha	2004 -	
Rohmer, Maureen	1989 - 1999	
Scherer, Arthur	1978 - 1983	
Schnakenberg, Henry	1956 - 1970	
Schneider, Kurt P.	1979 - 1985	
Schultz, Karen	1990 - 1999	
Shepard, Rodney P.	1931 - 1941	
Sipherd, Ray	1983 - 1989	
Sirois, Paul	2007 -	
Smith, JoAnn*	1990 - 1992	
Smith, Mortimer	1942 - 1960	
Smith, Scudder	1977 - 1982	
Spiro, Chris	1994 - 1999	
Stephan, Paula	2001 -	
Stephens, Ella H.	1954 - 1966	
Stern, Julie	1975 - 1976	
Stern, Peter	2004 -	
Stokes, Caroline	1974 - 1991	
Strook, Bertram A.	1974 - 1977	
Sturdevant, Richard	1996 - 2004	
Swanberg, William	1959 - 1980	
Telfair, Carole	1980 - 1989	
Tendler, Bob	1994 - 1995	
Tepas, Kevin	1995 - 2000	
Thomas, Mary	1988 - 1999	2000 -
Tiemann, Louise M.	1931 - 1938	
Toll, Susan	1959 - 1971	

Travis, Charles   1976 - 1980
Trentacosta, John   2006 -
Urso, Kelly   2004 -
Valenta, Kaaren   1997 - 2004
Warner, John   1987 - 1992
Warner, Margaret   1960 - 1975
Wheeler, Ruth S.   1931 - 1938
White Carolyn C.   1966 - 1969
Williams, Gordon   1988 - 1999   2001 - 2007
Wilson, Liz*   1982 - 1987
Wright, Frank   1931 - 1939
Wright, Mabel   1945 - 1955
Zang, Joanne   1979 - 1985   1996 - 2005
Zolov, Eleanor   1989 - 1994

Appendix D

Officers of the Newtown Library Association

President
E. L. Johnson - 1976- 1877
Marcus C. Hawley - 1877 - 1878
Daniel G. Beers - 1878 - 1880
Marcus C. Hawley - 1880 - 1884
Rev. John A. Crockett - 1884 - 1885
Professor C. S. Platt - 1886 -1896
Arthur S. Hawley - 1896-1897
Samuel J. Botsford - 1897 - 1899
Rev. George T. Linsley - 1899 - 1902
Rev. O. W. Barker - 1902 - 1905
Rev. James H. George - 1905 - 1917
Arthur G. Muzzy - 1917 - 1918

Rev. O.O. Wright - 1918 - 1919
Rev. E.O. Grisbrook - 1919 - 1923
Judge P.H. McCarthy - 1923 - 1934

Vice President
Charles Beresford - 1877 - 1882
Rev. G.M. Wilkins - 1882- 1884
Mr. Edgar F. Hawley - 1884 - 1886
Reuben H. Smith - 1886 - 1887
William A. Leonard - 1887 -1892
Rev. G. T. Linsley - 1892 -1899
Rev. O. W. Barker - 1899 - 1902
Rev. J. H. George - 1902 - 1905
Rev. R. E. Danforth - 1905 - 1907
Dr. Frank J. Gale - 1907 - 1918
Rev. E .O. Grisbrook - 1918 - 1919
H. Carleton Hubbell - 1919 - 1922
Dr. E. L. Kingman - 1922 - 1934

Secretary
Mary E. Beers - 1977 - 1882
Effie Glover - 1882 - 1887
Miss Emma Terrill - 1887- 1898
Mrs. Charles S. Platt - 1898 - 1908
Fannie Daniels - 1908 - 1910
Mrs. William Hawley - 1910 - 1915
Ada B. Blakeman - 1915 - 1927
John J. Northrop - 1927 - 1934

Treasurer
Mary C. Morgan - 1877 -1889
Charles H. Northrop - 1889 -1899
Arthur T. Nettleton - 1899 - 1908
Arthur J. Smith - 1908 - 1923
Charles F. Cavanaugh - 1923 - 1934

Assistant Treasurer
Miss Leonard - 1887-1888
Mrs. Charles S. Platt - 1887-1888

Librarian
Mary E. Beers - 1877 – 1878 - secretary and librarian
Charlotte Nichols - 1878 - 1887
Mrs. John C. Gay - 1887-1889
Miss Abbie Peck - 1889 - 1928
Ebba Moller - 1928 - 1931
Evelyn Pinkham - 1931 - 1934

INDEX

A

Alphabet of Zoar, 52
American Library Association, 1, 25-26
Angel, Henry, 88
Angel, John, 87
Angel, Laurence, 88
Antiques Reference Library, 112–113
Arcadia, 51
Art collection, 87–88
Antiques and the Arts Weekly, 112
Attenburg, Grosvenor, 22

B

Baier, Norman, 100
Baker, A.G., 110
Baldwin, Caleb, 1, 35
Baldwin, Sarah, 1–2
Balcony House, 70
Barker, Rev. Otis W., 21, 24
Baumer, Ed, 102
Beach, Isaac, 35
Beach, John Francis, 23
Beach, John Kimberly, 23–24
Beach Library, *see* John Beach Library Building
Beach, Rev. John, 20–24, 35
Beach, Rebecca, 18–21, 23–25
Beardsley, Mrs. C.F., 35
Beardsley, Josephine Lake, *see* Beardsley, Mrs. C.F.
Beers, Daniel G., 4
Beers, Mary E., 5–6
Bemis, Frederick, 50–52
Bemis, Isabelle, 50–52
Betts, Anna May, 49
Betts, Dr. Ralph, 49
Betts family store, 45
Bibliomation, 114
Blakeman, Austin, 46
Blakeman, Helen MacGregor fund, 37, 40
Bliss, Mrs. David, 86
Board of School Visitors, 3

Book Committee, 8
Book Nook, 111
Booth, Dr. Cyrenius H., 40, 60–61
Booth, Mary, 60
Booth, Sarah, 60, 111
Booth, William, 60
Boyd, Mary A., 50
Bowler, Diane, 108
Brew, Thomas F., 61
Briscoe, Alice E., 37
Brush, Chester, 85
Brush Genealogical Collection, 85, 93
Brush, Julia, 85
By-laws and rules for operation, 3

C

Carroll, Alice, 67, 105
Casella, Robert, 104
Chambers, Misses, 50
Charles H. Peck Collection, 70
Chase, Mrs. Julia A., 35
Christ's Episcopal Church, 20
Civil War Artifacts, 35–36
Clark, Abel, 37
Clark, Dennis, 95, 108
Clark, Homer, 51
Clark, Robert & Emeline, 85
Cliff, principal, 17
Collection, Artifacts, 36, 70–71
Colonial Dames of America, 47
Committee of Safety, 20
Community School, 57
Conti, Elizabeth, 113
Congregational Church, 20
Cookbook, Sarah Booth, 111
Crockett, Rev. John, 10–11
Cruson, Dan, 16n
Curator, Library, 71
Cyrenius H. Booth Library
  Setting the stage, 27–28
  Artifacts, 36–37
  Accessibility, 49
  Sandy Hook Library, 49–50
  Mary Hawley will, 55–56, 65

Library committee, 61
Construction, 62–67
Board of Trustees, 67–69
Historical collections, 69–71
Hawley Trust Fund, 82, 104
Julia Brush Collection, 85–87
John Angel Art Collection, 87–88
Expansion and modernization, 99–106
Lawsuits, 102, 110
Friends book sale, 106–112
Antiques Reference library, 112–113
Technology, effects of, 114–118
Cyrenius H. Booth Library Fund, 55. *See also* Hawley Trust Fund

D
Danbury Public Library, 86
DAR, 86
Davidson, Alice Hancock, 74–80
Dewey Decimal System, 33
Dewey, Melvil, 1, 29, 33
Dexter, Gladys B., 80–81
Dikeman, Mrs. Oscar, 34
Downs, Elizabeth "Betty," 92, 94–95, 108

E
Edmond, Judge William, 58, 60
Edmond, Sarah (Mrs. C.H. Booth), 60
Edmond Town Hall, 13, 58–59, 61
Erskine-Danforth Company, 63

F
Fairchild, Elmer W., 21, 37, 40
Fairfield Hills Hospital, 104, 110
Falconer, Bruce, 100
Ferris, Hilda, 93
Fires
  John Beach Library, 39
  Newtown Academy, 56
  Sandy Hook, 44–45
Fosdick, Raymond, 82
Free Public Library Issue, 4–5

Friends of the C.H. Booth Library, 106–112
Friends of the Library Book Sale, 116–112
Frost, Alex, 100

G
Gallagher & Schoenardt, 100
Gay, Mrs. John C., 7, 12
Gas rationing, 48, 77
Genealogy Research, 85–87
Glover Hall, 46, 48–49, 53
Glover, S.P., 45
Glover, William, 43
Golden Tea, 13
Goodrich, Al, 109–110
Grand Central Hotel, 25
Gray's Plain School, 50
Gray's Plain School War, 16
Griss, Steve, 101
Gushee, Anne, 108

H
Hadfield, Edward G., 41
Hadley, Arthur Twining, 50, 52
Hall, Irving Wheeler, 51–54
Hall's tin ship, 45
Hancock, Alice P. *See* Davidson, Alice Hancock
Harrison, Beryl, 113, 116
Harvard, John, 2
Hawley, Mary bedroom, 66
Hawley, Mary dining room, 66
Hawley Family Society, 56
Hawley Hardware, 4
Hawley, Marcus, 3, 10, 60–61
Hawley, Mary Elizabeth, 4, 56, 58, 60
  C.H. Booth Library, 28, 40
  Divorce, 11
  Furniture, 65–66
  Edmond Town Hall, 40, 58
  Hawley School, 40, 57
  Monument, 59
  Philanthropy, 57
  Scandal, 10

Village Cemetery, 57
Wedding, 10
Will, 55, 59, 62, 65, 81
Hawley, Sarah Booth, 10, 56, 60–61
Hawley, Thomas, 4
Hawley Trust Fund, 82, 104. *See Also* Cyrenius H. Booth Library Fund
Helen Blakeman Memorial Fund, 37, 30
Hensley, Dan, 36
Hensley, Mont, 36
Historical memorabilia, 70
Holian, Thomas, 61
Hosack, Dr., 60
Hoyt, Sarah Juliet, 37
Hubbell, Herbert C., 61, 67, 69

I
InfoTrac, 116
Inn at Newtown, 61
Internet, 116–117
Irvin, Rea, 90
Irish/Protestant Split, 15
Irish/Yankee Factions, 15

J
J. Donovan Associates, 102
Jewel, Professor, 33
John Beach Library Building, 19–25, 28, 37–40
Johnson, Dr. Samuel, 20
Johnson, Eliza Jane Camp, 3
Johnson, Ezra L., 2, 4, 60–61
Johnson, Frank, 88
Julia Brush Genealogical Collection, 85–87

K
Kearns, Jim, 106
King and Tuttle Feasibility Study, 102
Kingsbury, F. J., 24

L
Lauder, Harry, 51–52
Lawsuits, library, 102, 110
Lee, Anne, 114
Leeds Traveling Library #20, 47
Levi Morris' general store, 52
Library Fair, 13
Lighting Fund, 39
Linsley, Rev. George T., 19–20, 25, 28
Lucas, Mary, 83–84, 86, 107

M
Maskell, Jackie, 115
Masonic Hall, 43, 45
Mead, Sanford, 61
Mitchell, Mary, 109–110
Mitchell, Sarah, 78, 80, 84, 107
Moore & Salisbury Architects, 100
Morris, Charles G., 52, 61, 67
Morris, Levi, 52, 61
Morris, Mrs. Luzon, 50
Mulford, Stockton, 89
Museum, library, 36, 64

N
Nettleton, Arthur T., 20–21
  Advisor to Mary Hawley, 57
  Library Planning, 61–62
  C.H. Booth Library officer, 67–68
  Charles H. Peck Collection, 70
  Resignation from library board, 82
  Flagpole dedication, 83
  Death of, 83
Newtown Academy, 14, 26, 56
Newtown Bee, The
  Establishment date, 2
  Columns of Ezra Johnson, 2–3
  Letters to, 14, 100
  Library Association reports, 17
  John Beach Library Building, 24–26
  John Beach library funding, 39
  Sandy Hook library funding, 48

Irving Hall performance, 52–53
Mary Hawley will, 55
William Strong firing, 69
Indexing of, 93
Antiques Reference Library, 112
Newtown's first historian, 3
Newtown's first librarian, 6
Newtown Library Association, 3–18, 21–22, 25–27, 37, 40–41
Newtown Inn, 58, 62
Newtown Savings Bank, 4, 20, 57, 61
Newtown Trails Book, 109
Niantic Mill, 45
Nichols, Mrs. Charlotte, 6, 9
North District School, 24

O
Old Folk's Concert, 13

P
Parsons, Birdsey, 50
Peck, Abbie, 12, 37
Peck, Charles Henry, 70
Peck, Hannah, 70
Perry, Dr. Bennett, 60
Platt, Charles L., 11–14, 18
Platt, Fanny, 11
Platt, William, 11

R
Rationing, Gas, 48, 77
Ram Pasture, 62
Raynolds, Marguerite, 75
Raynolds, Robert, 75
Red Brick Building, 6, 112
ReQuest, 116
Resolutions, Association 1903, 26–27
Reverend John Beach Fund, 40–41
Rosenthal, Herb, 104
Ross, Harold, 90

S
Sandy Hook, 44
Sandy Hook Athletic Club, 48

Sandy Hook Fire Company, 45, 48
Sandy Hook Free Public Library, 17, 43, 46, 48–49
Sandy Hook Post Office, 43, 45, 48
Sanford, George P., 20
Sanford, Henry, 60
Sanford, Capt. Julius, 35
Sarah Booth Cookbook, 111
Schnakenberg, Henry, 88–91
Second Old Folk's Concert, 13
Shepard, Rodney, 61, 67
Smith, Allison P., 14, 93
Smith, R. Scudder, 112
Sniffen, Postmaster, 45
Soldiers and Sailors Monument, 21, 59
St. John's Church, 14, 43, 46
St. Rose Church, 14
Stoddard, Mr., 78
Stokes, Caroline, 49, 71
Strong, William N., 68
Strook, Bertram, 101
Subscription Library, 4–6
Sunderland, Philip, 58, 62–63
Sword, Capt. Sanford's, 35–36

T
Technology, 114-118
Television, effects of, 84
Thompson, Mrs. S.S., 35
Thurber, James, 90–91
Town Hall, Edmond, 13, 58–59, 61
Tracy, Vera, 68, 73
Trails Book, Newtown, 109
Traveling libraries, 47
  Leed's Traveling Library #20, 47
  Colonial Dames of America, 47
  District schoolhouses, 47, 75–76
Trinity Church, 10, 12, 20
Troy, Ed, 52
Tucker, Mrs. Nellie, 44

UV
Upham, William, 110
Upper Rubber Factory, 45
Village Cemetery, 57

W

Warner, John, 109
Wasserman, Julia, 104
Whist parties, 46
WiFi access, 117
Wiley, Mrs. L.J., 50
Wilkins, Rev. Morris, 10
Wireless Access, 117
World War II, effects of, 76
Woycik, Janet, 95–96, 117
Wright, Frank, 14
Wright, Rev. Otis O., 14-17, 43–44, 46

XYZ

Yale University, 62
Zang, Joanne, 107-109
Zimmermann, Andrea, 113
Zoar Library, 50

DANIEL CRUSON is a retired high school teacher who designed and taught courses in anthropology and local history. His abiding interest in these fields has led him to do extensive research and writing on the history of the towns of central Fairfield County including Easton, Redding, and Newtown as well as conducting archaeological investigations to learn more about the lifestyles of their past citizens, both historic and prehistoric. His attempts have led him to investigate deeply the subjects of rural slavery, vintage photography, early Connecticut architecture, colonial and post-colonial road building, and early cemeteries and their grave markers.

Mr. Cruson is active in a number of organizations dedicated to the research and preservation of local history. He has been a member of the historical society in Newtown where he lives, for 30 years, is active with The Heritage Preservation Trust of Newtown, Society of American Archeology, and The Archaeological Society of Connecticut for which he is currently serving as president. He is also the Town Historian for Newtown and served as the Chairman of the Newtown Tercentennial Commission in 2005.

He has published several books including *The Prehistory of Fairfield County*, *A Mosaic of Newtown History*, and most recently *The Slaves of Central Fairfield County*.